HOW ROMANTIC ARE YOU?

Answer *yes* or *no*

1. Do you often fall in love?
2. When you are in love, does your love absorb all your energies?
3. Do you work better when you are in love?
4. Do you think that being in love is essential for good sex?
5. Can you remember your first kiss?
6. Do you believe in love at first sight?
7. Do you cry at weepy movies?
8. Do you like buying or receiving flowers?
9. Would you enjoy a candlelit dinner for two at a country inn?
10. Do you carry a photo of your partner in your wallet?
11. Do you know the color of your lover's eyes?
12. Can you remember the date when you first met?
13. Can you remember what you were wearing?
14. Can you remember what your lover was wearing?
15. Do you like being in love?

Score one point for each *yes* answer.

If you scored from 9 to 15, you are a real old-fashioned romantic.
If you scored between 4 and 8, then love does play a part in your life, but you aren't one of the world's greatest romantics.
If you scored 3 or less, you aren't very romantic at all.

KNOW YOURSELF

Vernon Coleman

FAWCETT CREST • NEW YORK

A Fawcett Crest Book
Published by Ballantine Books
Copyright © 1988 by Vernon Coleman

ISBN 0-449-21778-7

Printed in Canada

First Ballantine Books Edition: October 1989

16   15   14   13   12   11   10   9   8

Contents

PART TWO

Introduction

There are 940 questions in *Know Yourself*—all carefully designed to enable you to find out as much as possible about yourself, to help you understand your own attitudes and motives, and to help you understand the attitudes and behavior of others. *Know Yourself* will enable you to make the best of your life and your relationships with other people.

Know Yourself is divided into two parts. Part One consists of forty-nine quizzes about your personality and attitudes. Part Two is designed to help you use the information you've gathered in Part One in a practical way. For example, Part One of the book will tell you whether you are assertive, loyal or romantic, while Part Two will tell you what sort of friend you are, what type of job would be right for you, whether you'd make a good political leader and whether or not you'd survive on a desert island!

It is vitally important that you read every question carefully before answering. For example, if a question asks if you would be "terribly embarrassed" if such and such happened, answer yes only if you would be *terribly* embarrassed. You will probably find that you can answer yes or no to most of the questions quite easily. If you do have difficulty in making a decision about which way to answer a particular question, think carefully and provide the answer that is the nearest approximation to the truth. The large number of questions in each questionnaire will ensure that you still obtain an accurate result.

Remember, too, that there are no ''right'' or ''wrong'' answers. The only rule is that you must always answer honestly. There is no point at all in cheating! The object of this book, after all, is to help you learn to know yourself.

Vernon Coleman
Barnstaple, Devon
1988

PART ONE

How optimistic are you?

Are you an optimist or a pessimist? Do you look at life through rose-colored spectacles or through dark glasses? Answer yes or no to each question.

1. If you heard a knock on your door late at night would you assume that it meant either bad news or trouble of some sort? ☐
2. Do you routinely carry safety pins and string with you in case something breaks? ☐
3. Do you ever bet? ☐
4. Do you ever dream about what you would do if you suddenly won or inherited a fortune? ☐
5. Do you always carry a raincoat or an umbrella with you when you go out? ☐
6. Do you spend a hefty part of your income on insurance? ☐
7. Would you ever go on holiday without first making hotel reservations? ☐
8. Do you think that most people are basically honest? ☐
9. If, when planning a holiday, you were going to leave your house key with a friend or neighbor, would you lock away valuables? ☐

10. Do you invariably feel enthusiastic about new projects? ☐

11. Would you lend money to an acquaintance who promised to pay you back? ☐

12. When planning a picnic or barbecue, do you always work out what you'll do if it rains? ☐

13. By and large do you trust people? ☐

14. If you had an important appointment, would you set off earlier than necessary to allow time for breakdowns or other delays? ☐

15. If your doctor arranged a hospital appointment for you, would you assume that something serious must be wrong? ☐

16. Do you invariably get up in the morning looking forward to the day ahead? ☐

17. Do you enjoy receiving unexpected letters and parcels? ☐

18. By and large, do you spend your money as it comes in—and let the future look after itself? ☐

19. Do you usually buy life insurance before travelling in an airplane? ☐

20. Are you looking forward to the next twelve months of your life? ☐

CHECK YOUR SCORE

1.	yes	0	no	1
2.	yes	0	no	1
3.	yes	1	no	0
4.	yes	1	no	0
5.	yes	0	no	1
6.	yes	0	no	1

7.	yes	1	no	0
8.	yes	1	no	0
9.	yes	0	no	1
10.	yes	1	no	0
11.	yes	1	no	0
12.	yes	0	no	1
13.	yes	1	no	0
14.	yes	0	no	1
15.	yes	0	no	1
16.	yes	1	no	0
17.	yes	1	no	0
18.	yes	1	no	0
19.	yes	0	no	1
20.	yes	1	no	0

Total =

If you scored 0 to 7, you are a complete pessimist. You nearly always seem to look on the black side. The only real advantage of being a pessimist is that because you expect little from the world you are rarely likely to be disappointed. There are, however, many disadvantages to having such a pessimistic approach to life. You expect failure so much that you are unlikely ever to try new projects. And every time anything goes wrong in your life your attitude and pessimistic approach will ensure that your gloom deepens. Pessimism can lead to depression, confusion, fear, anger and frustration. The only real solution is to try to establish a more positive approach to everything that you do and everyone you meet. Even though you will risk occasional disappointments you will gain far more from your life than if you constantly nurture a cautious, negative approach.

If you scored 8 to 14, your attitude to life is fairly well balanced. But you could undoubtedly enhance your health and your prospects by learning to deal with life's natural ups and downs in a more positive, optimistic way.

If you scored 15 to 20, you are a real optimist. Your natural tendency is to tackle life head on and to brush aside disappointments and problems. Optimism is a healthy state but do remember that your attitude could lead you to bite off more than you can chew.

How much of a worrier are you?

Answer these questions to find out whether you are timid, nervous and prone to anxiety or relaxed, calm and able to cope with anything.

1. Do you get nervous if you are alone in the dark? ☐
2. Do you ever wish that you had less responsibility? ☐
3. Do you worry about what people think about you? ☐
4. Do you frequently "jump" when the telephone rings? ☐
5. Do you worry about little things? ☐
6. Do you worry about your health? ☐
7. Do you worry about money? ☐
8. Do you worry a lot about missing connections when you're travelling? ☐

9. Do you ever lie awake worrying when you should be going to sleep? ☐
10. Do you ever need to take sleeping tablets? ☐
11. Have you ever needed to take tranquillizers? ☐
12. Would you describe yourself as very self-conscious? ☐
13. Does your voice shake if you are angry or very nervous? ☐
14. Do you get embarrassed easily? ☐
15. Can you relax easily? ☐
16. Are you more prone to anxiety than most people you know? ☐
17. Would you say that you were nearly always worried about something? ☐
18. Do you get upset easily? ☐
19. Do you ever suffer from "panic attacks"? ☐
20. Do you feel like packing everything in and running away? ☐
21. Do you suffer from any physical symptoms—for example, indigestion, skin rash or the like—that are made worse by pressure and stress? ☐
22. Are you often annoyed by noise? ☐
23. Do you get easily irritated by petty administrators? ☐
24. Do you get upset when things go wrong or break down? ☐
25. Do you get upset if people laugh at you? ☐
26. At night do you usually check the front door several times before going to bed? ☐
27. Do you get nervous before going out to parties, dinners or other social gatherings? ☐
28. If friends are coming around, do you spend hours preparing things for them? ☐

29. Do you blush easily?   ☐
30. Do you dislike meeting new people?   ☐

CHECK YOUR SCORE

1.	yes	1	no	0
2.	yes	1	no	0
3.	yes	1	no	0
4.	yes	1	no	0
5.	yes	1	no	0
6.	yes	1	no	0
7.	yes	1	no	0
8.	yes	1	no	0
9.	yes	1	no	0
10.	yes	1	no	0
11.	yes	1	no	0
12.	yes	1	no	0
13.	yes	1	no	0
14.	yes	1	no	0
15.	yes	0	no	1
16.	yes	1	no	0
17.	yes	1	no	0
18.	yes	1	no	0
19.	yes	1	no	0
20.	yes	1	no	0
21.	yes	1	no	0
22.	yes	1	no	0
23.	yes	1	no	0
24.	yes	1	no	0
25.	yes	1	no	0
26.	yes	1	no	0
27.	yes	1	no	0

28.	yes	1	no	0
29.	yes	1	no	0
30.	yes	1	no	0

Total =

A score of 10 or more suggests that you are a real worrier—the greater your score, the more of a worrier you are. Your natural mental make-up means that you are exceptionally vulnerable to stress and pressure. You cannot change your susceptibility to anxiety but you can protect yourself considerably by learning how to relax your mind and your body, and by learning to put your fears into some sort of perspective. One of the quickest ways to relax your mind is to learn how to "daydream." When you have a quiet moment, lie down somewhere peaceful and close your eyes. Imagine that you are on a warm, sunny beach. Imagine that you can hear the waves on the sand and feel the sun on your body. Allow your mind and your body to relax thoroughly. Once you've mastered this technique you can devise your own daydreams and use them to help you deal with many types of stressful situations.

A score of 4 to 9 suggests that although you are pretty much in command, you are still vulnerable to moments of anxiety. You can improve your mental strength by learning how to relax more completely.

If you scored 3 or less, you are at peace with yourself and perfectly capable of coping with most of the problems life is likely to throw at you.

How sociable are you?

How shy are you? How tactful are you? How well do you get along with other people?

1. Do you usually make an effort to get along with people you don't like? □

2. Do you prefer a noisy, busy holiday resort to a quiet, peaceful one? □

3. Do you enjoy going to parties, discos and noisy pubs? □

4. Do you make friends easily when you go on holiday or are traveling? □

5. Are you always pleased to see friends if they pop in unexpectedly? □

6. Have you ever initiated a conversation with a stranger on a train? □

7. Do you like organizing parties, dinners? □

8. Do you have lots of friends and acquaintances? □

9. Do you prefer noisy, busy evenings to quiet ones spent at home? □

10. Do you enjoy games at parties? □

11. Do you know most of your neighbors by their first names? □

12. Do you enjoy taking part—rather than winning—when playing games? ☐

13. Do you prefer people to machines? ☐

14. Do you like helping other people? ☐

15. You're at a dinner party. Your hostess serves up a dish that you think is horrible. Would you eat it? ☐

16. Do you send Christmas cards to people you don't really like? ☐

17. Have you ever been described as "the life and soul of the party"? ☐

18. Do you like meeting new people? ☐

19. Do you feel comfortable when you walk into a room where you know hardly anyone? ☐

20. Do you like children? ☐

21. Do you prefer to write a letter rather than use the telephone? ☐

22. Do you make friends easily? ☐

23. Do you ever pretend you're not in if you see unwelcome visitors arriving? ☐

24. Do you often have more people staying with you than your home can comfortably contain? ☐

25. Do you worry a lot about what other people think about you? ☐

CHECK YOUR SCORE

1.	yes	1	no	0
2.	yes	1	no	0
3.	yes	1	no	0
4.	yes	1	no	0
5.	yes	1	no	0
6.	yes	1	no	0

7.	yes	1	no	0
8.	yes	1	no	0
9.	yes	1	no	0
10.	yes	1	no	0
11.	yes	1	no	0
12.	yes	1	no	0
13.	yes	1	no	0
14.	yes	1	no	0
15.	yes	1	no	0
16.	yes	1	no	0
17.	yes	1	no	0
18.	yes	1	no	0
19.	yes	1	no	0
20.	yes	1	no	0
21.	yes	0	no	1
22.	yes	1	no	0
23.	yes	0	no	1
24.	yes	1	no	0
25.	yes	1	no	0

Total =

If you scored between 16 and 25, you are truly a sociable creature. You love people, you love being with people and you are probably at your happiest when you are in a crowd.

If you scored between 8 and 15, you enjoy being with people but as far as hectic parties go you can take them or leave them. Your patience is not limitless and you're probably perfectly happy to spend an evening with one or two really close friends rather than at a dinner party or function of some kind. And if you find yourself alone for the evening, then you can cope perfectly well with that too.

If you scored 7 or less, you are something of a loner. You'd almost certainly rather curl up with a good book, sit yourself down in front of the TV or get on with some work rather than go out and make merry with a host of friends. You are self-sufficient and enjoy your own company.

How obsessive are you?

Are there strict patterns to your life? Are you driven and ruled by things that you have to do?

1. Would you describe yourself as a perfectionist? ☐
2. Are you, by nature, neat and tidy? ☐
3. Do you get upset if your daily habits are disrupted? ☐
4. Do you get annoyed if people borrow things and then don't put them back in their right places? ☐
5. Would you feel uncomfortable living in an untidy house? ☐
6. Do you find it difficult to delegate responsibility? ☐
7. Can you always account for every penny of your money? ☐
8. Do you stock up with supplies of essential food-stuffs in case there is ever a shortage? ☐
9. Do you regularly indulge in superstitious rituals, such as not stepping on cracked paving stones? ☐

10. Do you ever have recurrent thoughts that just won't leave your mind? ☐

11. Do you ever feel that you have to wash your hands a lot even though they're quite clean? ☐

12. Do you usually plump up the cushions on the sofa and chairs before going to bed at night? ☐

13. Do you like to keep your belongings neat and tidy looking? ☐

14. Do you like to get the washing-up done straight after a meal? ☐

15. Do you always check that everything is switched off before you go up to bed at night? ☐

16. If you walk into a room and see a picture hanging awry, do you have to straighten it? ☐

17. When having a meal, do you try to get the washing-up done between courses? ☐

18. If you give a party, after the guests leave, do you usually tidy up before you go to bed? ☐

19. Do you ever forget important dates? ☐

20. Are you forever "losing" important papers? ☐

21. Do you keep all your expenses receipts neatly filed? ☐

22. Do you usually know how much money you've got in your current account? ☐

23. Have you ever lost a key and locked yourself out of your house or car? ☐

24. Do you normally buy Christmas cards and presents well in advance? ☐

25. Do you hate to see ashtrays filled with cigarette ash? ☐

26. Do you always arrive early for trains and airplanes? ☐

27. Do you leave things behind when traveling or staying away from home? ☐

28. Could you put your hand on last year's tax return within sixty seconds? ☐
29. Do you feel ashamed or embarrassed if people see you wearing old or scruffy gardening clothes? ☐
30. Do you forget appointments or messages? ☐

CHECK YOUR SCORE

1.	yes	0	no	1
2.	yes	0	no	1
3.	yes	0	no	1
4.	yes	0	no	1
5.	yes	0	no	1
6.	yes	0	no	1
7.	yes	0	no	1
8.	yes	0	no	1
9.	yes	0	no	1
10.	yes	0	no	1
11.	yes	0	no	1
12.	yes	0	no	1
13.	yes	0	no	1
14.	yes	0	no	1
15.	yes	0	no	1
16.	yes	0	no	1
17.	yes	0	no	1
18.	yes	0	no	1
19.	yes	1	no	0
20.	yes	1	no	0
21.	yes	0	no	1
22.	yes	0	no	1
23.	yes	1	no	0
24.	yes	0	no	1

25.	yes	0	no	1
26.	yes	0	no	1
27.	yes	1	no	0
28.	yes	0	no	1
29.	yes	0	no	1
30.	yes	1	no	0

Total =

If you scored 0 to 8, your life is undoubtedly ruled by your obsessions. You are probably neat, tidy, punctual, reliable and cautious. Your personal life-style doesn't allow much room for excitement or emotional explosions and your obsessions may also lead others to call you dull or boring. However, you feel more comfortable with people who are responsible and careful and, with due regard to their sources, you probably regard such comments with some suspicion. You are likely to be an excellent, punctilious worker and although you're unlikely to set the world on fire, you're perfectly capable of doing your bit to help keep it turning round.

If you scored between 9 and 18, you can pride yourself on showing a mature balance between reliability and originality. You have a strong streak of responsibility running through your psychological make-up but you still know how to have fun. And you're perfectly capable of surprising people who think they know you.

If you scored 19 to 30, you are probably fairly unreliable, extremely untidy and frequently irresponsible. On the other hand, you are full of ideas and very likely to be the life and soul of any party. You are probably generous to your friends and although you may often find yourself in trouble of one sort or another you usually manage to survive somehow.

How absent-minded are you?

Is your head forever in the clouds or are your feet firmly planted on the floor?

1. Have you ever been accused of being "miles away"? ☐
2. Do you ever day dream? ☐
3. Have you ever driven past your turn-off on a motorway? ☐
4. Have you ever forgotten to get off a train or bus, and gone miles past your station or stop? ☐
5. Do you ever forget to eat? ☐
6. Do you ever forget your own car number? ☐
7. Do you ever forget your own telephone number? ☐
8. Do you spend time most days looking for things that you've lost? ☐
9. Do you ever not know what day of the week it is? ☐
10. Do you ever get to the front door and only then realize that it is pouring down with rain and you don't have a coat or umbrella? ☐
11. Do you ever call people by the wrong names? ☐

12. Do you ever forget where your car is parked? ☐
13. Have you ever forgotten an important birthday or anniversary? ☐
14. Have you ever turned up for an appointment on the wrong day? ☐
15. Have you ever written two letters and put them in the wrong envelopes? ☐
16. Do you habitually leave things behind at friends' homes and in restaurants and hotels? ☐
17. Have you ever put on someone else's coat when leaving a restaurant? ☐
18. Do you ever forget your own age? ☐
19. Have you ever got into a shop and forgotten what you wanted to buy? ☐
20. Have you ever put on odd shoes by mistake? ☐

CHECK YOUR SCORE

1.	yes	1	no	0
2.	yes	1	no	0
3.	yes	1	no	0
4.	yes	1	no	0
5.	yes	1	no	0
6.	yes	1	no	0
7.	yes	1	no	0
8.	yes	1	no	0
9.	yes	1	no	0
10.	yes	1	no	0
11.	yes	1	no	0
12.	yes	1	no	0
13.	yes	1	no	0
14.	yes	1	no	0

15.	yes	1	no	0
16.	yes	1	no	0
17.	yes	1	no	0
18.	yes	1	no	0
19.	yes	1	no	0
20.	yes	1	no	0

Total =

If you scored between 8 and 20, you are a dreamer—probably full of ideas but often apparently detached from the real world. Your friends and relatives are probably frequently exasperated by your poor memory and general absent-mindedness. Actually, you may well have quite a good memory, but there is so much going on in your head that you aren't always aware of what is going on around you. One thing that probably annoys your friends and relatives a good deal is your tendency to ignore questions that you've been asked. You may well make things worse by offering an answer minutes later, proving that you had at least heard the question but that your mind had been on other matters.

If you scored between 5 and 7, you have one foot planted firmly on the ground, but you do have a slight tendency to drift off occasionally.

If you scored 4 or less, you have both feet planted very firmly on the ground. You are reliable, well organized, responsible and certainly not absent-minded.

How assertive are you?

Do you stand up for yourself or do you lie down and get trodden on?

1. You buy a car. A week later it breaks down. Would you complain? ☐
2. If you saw someone cruelly beating a dog in the street, would you interfere? ☐
3. You are on a train in a no smoking compartment. Someone lights a cigarette. Would you say anything? ☐
4. Your boss introduces a silly rule at work. Would you object? ☐
5. Do you find it difficult to walk away from people who are annoying or boring you? ☐
6. Do you find yourself explaining and excusing the things that you do? ☐
7. An acquaintance rings up and wants you to join a committee. You know it will be a boring waste of time. Would you have the courage to say "No, thank you" straight away? ☐
8. Would you find it easy to reject unwanted advice offered by a relative? ☐

9. In a shop a salesman goes to a lot of effort on your behalf. Would you feel obliged to buy something even if you hadn't found what you wanted? ☐

10. When you're on holiday do you waste time writing postcards to people you don't particularly like? ☐

11. Do you buy Christmas cards and presents for people you don't really like—just because they buy cards and presents for you? ☐

12. On the beach someone is playing a radio very loudly. Would you object? ☐

13. A neighbor's dog is barking loudly. Would you call round to complain? ☐

14. You don't understand something that your doctor says. Would you ask him to explain? ☐

15. You are kept waiting to see someone even though you have an appointment. Would you object? ☐

16. You want to buy two batteries, but the batteries you want are sold in threes. Would you ask the shop assistant to split a pack for you? ☐

17. You are overcharged in a restaurant. Would you complain? ☐

18. In a hotel the bellboy insists on carrying your bag to your room even though it is light and you don't need him. Would you tip him? ☐

19. You order a rare steak in a restaurant. The waiter brings one that is well done. Would you complain? ☐

20. An old lady pushes ahead of you in a queue. Would you politely but firmly insist on regaining your place? ☐

21. You are on a diet. A friend insists on buying you a cake? Would you eat it? ☐

22. Do you regularly find yourself tidying up after other people? ☐

23. Someone you don't like makes a move to kiss you at a Christmas party. Would you accept the kiss? ☐

24. Your doctor tells you that you have a serious illness for which there is no cure. Would you ask for a second opinion? ☐

25. Are most of your decisions made for you by other people? ☐

26. The telephone rings while you are making love. Would you answer it? ☐

27. In a restaurant the service is poor. Would you still leave a tip? ☐

28. Someone telephones just as you are sitting down to a meal. Would you ask them to call back later? ☐

29. Do you invariably watch TV programs that other people want to watch? ☐

30. Do you ever find yourself lending things that you'd rather not lend—and regretting your action afterward? ☐

31. Would you complain if you thought that your bank had made a mistake? ☐

32. Would you send back wine that tasted sour? ☐

33. Do you write at least one letter of complaint every month? ☐

34. If a policeman was rude to you, would you take his number and complain about him? ☐

35. Do you usually get your own way? ☐

36. Do you usually try to tell people what you think they want to hear rather than what you really feel? ☐

37. Once you've made up your mind, do you usually stick to your decision? ☐

38. Are you easily intimidated by authority? □
39. Are you easily intimidated by people in uniform? □
40. Have you ever asked to see the manager in a restaurant or hotel? □

CHECK YOUR SCORE

1.	yes	1	no	0
2.	yes	1	no	0
3.	yes	1	no	0
4.	yes	1	no	0
5.	yes	0	no	1
6.	yes	0	no	1
7.	yes	1	no	0
8.	yes	1	no	0
9.	yes	0	no	1
10.	yes	0	no	1
11.	yes	0	no	1
12.	yes	1	no	0
13.	yes	1	no	0
14.	yes	1	no	0
15.	yes	1	no	0
16.	yes	1	no	0
17.	yes	1	no	0
18.	yes	0	no	1
19.	yes	1	no	0
20.	yes	1	no	0
21.	yes	0	no	1
22.	yes	0	no	1
23.	yes	0	no	1
24.	yes	1	no	0
25.	yes	0	no	1

26.	yes	0	no	1
27.	yes	0	no	1
28.	yes	1	no	0
29.	yes	0	no	1
30.	yes	0	no	1
31.	yes	1	no	0
32.	yes	1	no	0
33.	yes	1	no	0
34.	yes	1	no	0
35.	yes	1	no	0
36.	yes	0	no	1
37.	yes	1	no	0
38.	yes	0	no	1
39.	yes	0	no	1
40.	yes	1	no	0

Total =

If you scored between 25 and 40, you can stand up for yourself very well. You're certainly not the sort of person who gets pushed around. People who don't know you very well may regard you as being rude, overbearing or even boorish. But those who know you would probably say that you simply do not suffer fools and idiots very well. The higher your score, of course, the more assertive you are.

If you scored between 10 and 24, you can look after yourself and stand up for yourself, but much of the time you are far too polite to say what you think. As a result people probably do take advantage of you.

If you scored 9 or less, your life is probably being run for you by other people. As a result you will probably suffer a great deal from frustration and hidden anger. These feelings can easily affect your physical health. You need to stand your ground and protect your territory with more vigor. You don't have to be rude or unpleasant. Start by learning to be honest. You'll gain self-respect—and the respect of others. If you don't want to do something, then say so. If you have reason to complain, then swallow hard and complain. The more you do it, the easier it will become. You'll be surprised to find that people soon treat you with far more consideration.

How responsible are you?

Are you the sort of person your mother warned you not to mix with?

1. Are you usually on time for appointments? ☐
2. Would you describe yourself as reliable? ☐
3. Do you put money aside for the future? ☐
4. If you found out that friends of yours were involved in something illegal, would you tell the police? ☐
5. When out for the day, do you always take your rubbish home with you? ☐
6. Do you exercise regularly to keep your body healthy? ☐
7. Do you avoid ''junk'' foods, fats and other foodstuffs that are likely to be bad for you? ☐

8. Do you always try to put business before pleasure? ☐
9. Do you always vote in elections? ☐
10. Do you always reply to letters within a day or two of getting them? ☐
11. Do you believe the saying that "a job worth doing is worth doing well"? ☐
12. Do you invariably keep appointments—even if you're not feeling well? ☐
13. Have you ever been in trouble with the police? ☐
14. Were you a prefect or monitor when you were at school? ☐
15. As a child, did you regularly help around the house? ☐

CHECK YOUR SCORE

1.	yes	1	no	0
2.	yes	1	no	0
3.	yes	1	no	0
4.	yes	1	no	0
5.	yes	1	no	0
6.	yes	1	no	0
7.	yes	1	no	0
8.	yes	1	no	0
9.	yes	1	no	0
10.	yes	1	no	0
11.	yes	1	no	0
12.	yes	1	no	0
13.	yes	0	no	1
14.	yes	1	no	0
15.	yes	1	no	0

Total =

If you scored between 10 and 15, you are extremely responsible and sensible. You are careful, polite, reliable and probably honest too.

If you scored between 3 and 9, you can be responsible but you do have a strong streak of irresponsibility running through your life.

If you scored 2 or less, you are definitely the sort of person that most mothers don't like their children knowing. You probably lurch from crisis to crisis. You may have difficulty in keeping jobs and you are probably always short of money.

How dominating are you?

Are you a leader or a follower?

1. Do you find it difficult to say no when people ask you to do things? ☐
2. Do you avoid confrontations even when you think that you are right? ☐
3. Generally speaking, do you obey rules and regulations? ☐
4. Do you find yourself apologizing a good deal? ☐
5. If someone laughed at an item of clothing, would you avoid wearing it again? ☐

6. Do you always try to dress in a fashionable way? ☐
7. Do you ever wear clothes that make you look good even if they are uncomfortable? ☐
8. Do you ever make rude signs or gestures at other drivers? ☐
9. Do you get impatient with people who are slow to understand? ☐
10. Do you swear a lot? ☐
11. Do you ever make other people look ''small'' or stupid? ☐
12. Do you get very cross at opinions expressed on television? ☐
13. If a workman did a bad job, would you tell him that you weren't satisfied? ☐
14. Do you tend to speak your mind regardless of the consequences? ☐
15. Would you describe yourself as intolerant? ☐
16. Do you hate losing arguments? ☐
17. Do other people make most of your big decisions for you? ☐
18. Would you prefer to invest for security rather than growth? ☐
19. Do you dress in a way that is designed to attract attention? ☐
20. Do you feel comfortable if you're part of a crowd? ☐

CHECK YOUR SCORE

1.	yes	1	no	0
2.	yes	1	no	0
3.	yes	1	no	0
4.	yes	1	no	0

5.	yes	1	no	0
6.	yes	1	no	0
7.	yes	1	no	0
8.	yes	0	no	1
9.	yes	0	no	1
10.	yes	0	no	1
11.	yes	0	no	1
12.	yes	0	no	1
13.	yes	0	no	1
14.	yes	0	no	1
15.	yes	0	no	1
16.	yes	0	no	1
17.	yes	1	no	0
18.	yes	1	no	0
19.	yes	0	no	1
20.	yes	1	no	0

Total =

If you scored between 14 and 20, you are definitely a follower rather than a leader. You are more comfortable being told what to do than giving orders and instructions. In a crisis you would rather see someone else take charge—although you would be happy to do whatever you were asked to do.

If you scored between 7 and 13, you have a rather streaky personality. You can take the lead—and you feel quite happy telling others what to do—but on the whole you probably don't have that extra ounce of aggression that turns someone into a real leader.

If you scored 6 or less, you are a born leader. Your personality is so powerful that you probably feel extremely uncomfortable if given orders. If denied authority, you are likely to be something of a rebel.

Are you a doer or a thinker?

Do you talk about it and dream about it—or do you *do* it?

1. Do you like being busy? ☐
2. Do you get frustrated by slow-moving traffic? ☐
3. Do you tend to rush from place to place and job to job? ☐
4. Do you feel miserable when just sitting around? ☐
5. Do you prefer taking part to watching? ☐
6. Do you take the stairs if there is a wait for an elevator? ☐
7. Do people ever complain that you do things too quickly? ☐
8. Do you get up early even on weekends? ☐
9. Do you get very enthusiastic about new projects? ☐
10. Do you like organizing other people? ☐
11. Do you prefer action to planning? ☐
12. Do you spend a lot of time meditating and day-dreaming? ☐
13. Do you ever think about where we **all** came from—and why? ☐
14. Do you enjoy doing crossword puzzles? ☐
15. Do you enjoy visiting museums and art galleries? ☐

16. Do you enjoy good conversation?   ☐
17. Do you usually go up stairs two at a time?   ☐
18. Do you seem to get more things done than other people you know?   ☐
19. Do you prefer busy, active holidays to leisurely, relaxing holidays?   ☐
20. Do you get bored easily if you haven't got anything to do?   ☐

CHECK YOUR SCORE

1.	yes	1	no	0
2.	yes	1	no	0
3.	yes	1	no	0
4.	yes	1	no	0
5.	yes	1	no	0
6.	yes	1	no	0
7.	yes	1	no	0
8.	yes	1	no	0
9.	yes	1	no	0
10.	yes	1	no	0
11.	yes	1	no	0
12.	yes	0	no	1
13.	yes	0	no	1
14.	yes	0	no	1
15.	yes	0	no	1
16.	yes	0	no	1
17.	yes	1	no	0
18.	yes	1	no	0
19.	yes	1	no	0
20.	yes	1	no	0

Total =

If you scored 12 to 20, you are definitely a doer rather than a thinker. You prefer to be busy doing things rather than talking about them. You like being active and having plenty to do.

If you scored 6 to 11, you really do enjoy the best of both worlds: you enjoy being busy but you don't mind having time to think occasionally. You can adapt yourself fairly easily to a wide range of circumstances.

If you scored 5 or less, you are definitely a thinker. You much prefer sitting down with a book or just your thoughts to rushing around doing things. You can entertain yourself quite easily and although you enjoy good company and good conversation, you can manage quite well on your own.

How loyal are you?

Do you have a strong sense of loyalty? And where do your loyalties lie?

1. Do you put the needs of your job, employer or family above your own needs and wants? ☐
2. Do you feel really bad if you let someone down? ☐
3. Do you feel guilty if you need to have time off work because of illness? ☐

4. Do you worry about work when you are away on holiday? ☐

5. Do you think that your own happiness should always come first? ☐

6. Would you work over Christmas to help an employer? ☐

7. Would you die for your country? ☐

8. Would you die to save your family? ☐

9. If you found that a friend had been stealing, would you tell the police? ☐

10. If you found that your partner had been stealing, would you tell the police? ☐

11. If you found that your mother had been stealing, would you tell the police? ☐

12. If called up to serve in your country's armed forces, would your first reaction be to look for an opportunity to avoid joining up? ☐

13. Would you accept $1,000 to sell an employer's secret to a competitor? ☐

14. Would you sell an employer's secret to a competitor for $10,000? ☐

15. Would you sell an employer's secret to a competitor for $100,000? ☐

16. Would you sell an employer's secret to a competitor for $1,000,000? ☐

17. Would you accept $1,000 to betray your country to an enemy? ☐

18. Would you accept $10,000 to betray your country to an enemy? ☐

19. Would you accept $100,000 to betray your country to an enemy? ☐

20. Would you accept $1,000,000 to betray your country to an enemy?   □

CHECK YOUR SCORE

1.	yes	1	no	0
2.	yes	1	no	0
3.	yes	1	no	0
4.	yes	1	no	0
5.	yes	0	no	1
6.	yes	1	no	0
7.	yes	1	no	0
8.	yes	1	no	0
9.	yes	0	no	1
10.	yes	0	no	1
11.	yes	0	no	1
12.	yes	0	no	1
13.	yes	0	no	1
14.	yes	0	no	1
15.	yes	0	no	1
16.	yes	0	no	1
17.	yes	0	no	1
18.	yes	0	no	1
19.	yes	0	no	1
20.	yes	0	no	1

Total =

If you scored between 12 and 20, you are very much the loyal sort. You put others first and yourself last. You are selfless almost to a fault and you would make the sort of employee that any employer should be proud to have.

If you scored between 7 and 11, you are basically loyal but you can be tempted away from your loyalty—particularly by money or other rewards.

If you scored 6 or less, you put loyalty to others fairly low on your list. You may feel a strong sense of loyalty to very close friends or immediate relatives, but by and large you follow the philosophy of "every man for himself." Some would perhaps describe you as selfish, but you prefer to think of yourself as a realist.

How intuitive are you?

Did you know that I was going to ask this question?

1. Do you do well in guessing games? ☐
2. Have you ever had a run of good luck when gambling? ☐
3. Have you ever felt that a house was "right" or "happy" as soon as you saw it? ☐
4. Have you ever felt that you wanted to know someone better after seeing them for no more than an instant? ☐
5. Have you ever "known" who was at the other end before picking up a ringing telephone? ☐
6. Have you ever heard voices telling you what to do? ☐
7. Do you believe in fate? ☐

8. Do you ever know what people are going to say before they say it? □

9. Have you ever had a bad dream that turned out to be true? □

10. Have you ever known what was in a letter before opening it? □

11. Do you ever complete people's sentences for them? □

12. Have you ever thought about someone you haven't heard from for a while and then had a postcard, phone call or letter from, or met him or her quite unexpectedly? □

13. Do you inexplicably find yourself distrusting some people? □

14. Do you pride yourself on being able to judge people fairly accurately on first appearances? □

15. Have you experienced the phenomenon known as *déjà vu*? □

16. Have you ever refused to get on an airplane because you feared that it might crash? □

17. Have you ever woken up in the night worrying about the health or safety of a friend or relative? □

18. Do you dislike some people for no very good reason? □

19. Do you ever see an item of clothing and feel that you must have it? □

20. Do you believe there is any truth in the saying "love at first sight"?

CHECK YOUR SCORE

1.	yes	1	no	0
2.	yes	1	no	0

3.	yes	1	no	0
4.	yes	1	no	0
5.	yes	1	no	0
6.	yes	1	no	0
7.	yes	1	no	0
8.	yes	1	no	0
9.	yes	1	no	0
10.	yes	1	no	0
11.	yes	1	no	0
12.	yes	1	no	0
13.	yes	1	no	0
14.	yes	1	no	0
15.	yes	1	no	0
16.	yes	1	no	0
17.	yes	1	no	0
18.	yes	1	no	0
19.	yes	1	no	0
20.	yes	1	no	0

Total =

If you scored between 10 and 20, you have an extremely powerful sense of intuition. You have unusual skills and you aren't afraid to follow your instincts.

If you scored between 1 and 9, you do have a strong sense of intuition but you may not always make the most of your natural skills. Get into the habit of allowing your sense of intuition to make decisions for you. With minor decisions, learn to follow whatever thought springs first into your mind. If you have a difficult problem to solve, do something quite relaxing—take a walk or a bath, for example—and allow thoughts and ideas to drift into your mind. You'll be surprised at the number of possible solutions and answers that will occur to you. Write down all these possible answers and then look through the list carefully. You'll find that the best solutions will leap up at you.

If you scored 0 on this questionnaire, you have not allowed your sense of intuition to develop at all. But you have a sense of intuition hidden deep down in your mind. Try to get into the habit of allowing your instincts to take over. The chances are high that you'll soon find yourself enjoying all the advantages of a healthy and strong sense of intuition.

How imaginative are you?

Do you have wings? Do you enjoy an occasional flight of fancy?

1. Do you ever dream when you are asleep? ☐
2. Do you daydream when you should be doing other things? ☐
3. Do you ever get nightmares? ☐
4. Do you ever have fantasies about celebrities? ☐
5. Do you have any strong religious views? ☐
6. Do you ever get frightened when watching horror movies? ☐

7. Do you ever wonder what it would be like to live in a different century? ☐
8. Do you ever worry about the safety of close friends or relatives when they are traveling? ☐
9. Do you ever fantasize when making love? ☐
10. Do you believe in ghosts? ☐
11. Do you believe that flying saucers have landed on Earth? ☐
12. Do you believe in fairies? ☐
13. Could you write a novel? ☐
14. Do you believe that it is possible to communicate with the dead? ☐
15. Do you believe that there could be huge monsters alive at the bottom of the sea? ☐
16. Do you ever plan what you would do if you won a million dollars? ☐
17. Do you ever talk back to the radio or the television? ☐
18. Do you ever conduct music in your own home? ☐
19. Do you ever mentally undress members of the opposite sex? ☐
20. Do you believe in reincarnation? ☐

CHECK YOUR SCORE

1.	yes	1	no	0
2.	yes	1	no	0
3.	yes	1	no	0
4.	yes	1	no	0
5.	yes	1	no	0
6.	yes	1	no	0
7.	yes	1	no	0
8.	yes	1	no	0

9.	yes	1	no	0
10.	yes	1	no	0
11.	yes	1	no	0
12.	yes	1	no	0
13.	yes	1	no	0
14.	yes	1	no	0
15.	yes	1	no	0
16.	yes	1	no	0
17.	yes	1	no	0
18.	yes	1	no	0
19.	yes	1	no	0
20.	yes	1	no	0

Total =

If you scored between 8 and 20, you have a well-developed imagination.

If you scored between 3 and 7, your imagination is struggling to make itself heard. Stop suppressing it. Allow your imagination to take over occasionally.

If you scored 2 or less, you have succeeded in crushing your imagination. You will add a new and pleasant dimension to your life if you can allow your imagination to develop.

How vulnerable are you to guilty feelings?

Are you riddled with self-doubt or full of self-confidence?

1. Do you worry a lot about what other people think? ☐
2. Do you feel bad if you go into a shop and come out without buying anything? ☐
3. Do you avoid doing things that might upset other people? ☐
4. If someone saw you naked—by mistake—would you be mortified? ☐
5. Do you find it difficult to lie in bed on a Sunday morning? ☐
6. Do you ever send Christmas cards to people you don't like very much? ☐
7. Do you ever give Christmas or birthday presents to people you don't like? ☐
8. Do you invariably choose your clothes to please other people? ☐
9. Do you feel really bad if you let people down? ☐
10. Do you spend a lot of your life doing things that you don't really enjoy? ☐
11. Do you often apologize when in fact it isn't your fault? ☐

12. Do you think that you have disappointed your parents? ☐

13. Have you ever committed an unforgivable sin? ☐

14. Do you often feel ashamed? ☐

15. Do you find it easy to forget when you've done something wrong? ☐

16. Do you usually blame yourself when things go wrong with relationships? ☐

17. Do you have any regrets that will stay with you for the rest of your life? ☐

18. Do you expect to be punished by God for your sins? ☐

19. Are you sometimes disgusted by your sexual feelings or fantasies? ☐

20. Are you sometimes disgusted by other people's sexual feelings or fantasies? ☐

21. Are you embarrassed when you hear dirty stories? ☐

22. Do you regularly pray for forgiveness? ☐

23. Were your teachers disappointed in your work at school? ☐

24. Do you often think back on how badly you behaved in the past? ☐

25. Do you have a guilty secret that will come out one day? ☐

26. Are you bothered by pangs of conscience? ☐

27. Are you full of regrets about your early sexual life? ☐

28. Do you have some inexcusable habits? ☐

29. Do you think that you get more love and affection than you deserve? ☐

30. Do you spend a lot of time going over things in your past? ☐

CHECK YOUR SCORE

1.	yes	1	no	0
2.	yes	1	no	0
3.	yes	1	no	0
4.	yes	1	no	0
5.	yes	1	no	0
6.	yes	1	no	0
7.	yes	1	no	0
8.	yes	1	no	0
9.	yes	1	no	0
10.	yes	1	no	0
11.	yes	1	no	0
12.	yes	1	no	0
13.	yes	1	no	0
14.	yes	1	no	0
15.	yes	0	no	1
16.	yes	1	no	0
17.	yes	1	no	0
18.	yes	1	no	0
19.	yes	1	no	0
20.	yes	1	no	0
21.	yes	1	no	0
22.	yes	1	no	0
23.	yes	1	no	0
24.	yes	1	no	0
25.	yes	1	no	0
26.	yes	1	no	0
27.	yes	1	no	0
28.	yes	1	no	0
29.	yes	1	no	0
30.	yes	1	no	0

Total =

If you scored between 15 and 30, your life is, to a very considerable extent, influenced by one of the most powerful and damaging of human emotions—guilt. Most of us have an inbuilt sense of right and wrong and if we trespass against it, we feel guilty. This inbuilt sense of right and wrong—conscience, if you like—does not come from some mysterious inherited force but from social and religious prejudices that have been established by instruction and example. We feel guilty because we fail to live up to the expectations of those around us. This internally inspired pressure is impossible to escape and extremely damaging. Guilt is responsible for much physical and mental illness. In order to counteract your feelings of inadequacy and guilt, and build up your self-assurance, you need to learn to think of yourself as a success. Try preparing an advertisement for yourself, listing all your skills and virtues. When next you feel ashamed of your inadequacies, try to think instead of your strengths. Accept your limitations and your faults but temper this with the realization that your limitations have limits.

If you scored between 8 and 14, guilt still plays a part in your life—although you are certainly not submerged by feelings of inadequacy.

If you scored 7 or less, you are brimming with self-confidence. Guilt does not play a large part in your life.

How emotional are you?

Are you uptight? Or loose, cool and ready to let it all hang out?

1. Do you feel guilty if you cry in public? ☐
2. Do you think that crying is a sign of weakness? ☐
3. Do you think that men and boys should be encouraged to hide their tears? ☐
4. Do you feel embarrassed if you find yourself crying while watching a film or reading a book? ☐
5. Would you try to hold back your tears if you were attending a funeral? ☐
6. Would you distrust a politician who shed tears in public? ☐
7. Do you think that tears are an unnecessary expression of emotion? ☐
8. Would you allow someone to comfort you if you were found crying? ☐
9. Do you get embarrassed if you see grown men crying? ☐
10. Would you pretend that you had something in your eye if you were unexpectedly discovered crying? ☐
11. Do you always try to hide your anger? ☐
12. Do you always try to hide your disappointment? ☐

13. Does your temper ever get out of control? ☐

14. Has your temper ever got you into trouble? ☐

15. Do you believe that it does you good to get rid of your anger? ☐

16. Do you tend to brood about things which have made you angry? ☐

17. Do you get cross quite easily? ☐

18. Do you touch someone you love at least once a day? ☐

19. Do you enjoy physical signs of affection? ☐

20. Do you ever get broody when you see small babies? ☐

21. Would you happily hold hands in public with someone you cared for? ☐

22. Do you enjoy being massaged? ☐

23. Do you regularly tell those whom you love how you feel? ☐

24. Have you ever had a pet of which you were very fond? ☐

25. Do you enjoy being kissed and hugged by people you love? ☐

26. Do you ever laugh out loud when you are watching funny films? ☐

27. Do you ever tap your feet while listening to music? ☐

28. Do you often have the last clap at concerts, sports events and the like? ☐

29. Do you ever shout encouragement to sports or TV heroes? ☐

30. Can you remember when you last really laughed and enjoyed yourself? ☐

CHECK YOUR SCORE

1.	yes	0	no	1
2.	yes	0	no	1
3.	yes	0	no	1
4.	yes	0	no	1
5.	yes	0	no	1
6.	yes	0	no	1
7.	yes	0	no	1
8.	yes	1	no	0
9.	yes	0	no	1
10.	yes	0	no	1
11.	yes	0	no	1
12.	yes	0	no	1
13.	yes	1	no	0
14.	yes	1	no	0
15.	yes	1	no	0
16.	yes	0	no	1
17.	yes	1	no	0
18.	yes	1	no	0
19.	yes	1	no	0
20.	yes	1	no	0
21.	yes	1	no	0
22.	yes	1	no	0
23.	yes	1	no	0
24.	yes	1	no	0
25.	yes	1	no	0
26.	yes	1	no	0
27.	yes	1	no	0
28.	yes	1	no	0
29.	yes	1	no	0
30.	yes	1	no	0

Total =

If you scored between 17 and 30, your attitude towards your emotions is a healthy one. You aren't ashamed to let your emotions show occasionally, and you will undoubtedly be much healthier because of this attitude.

If you scored between 8 and 16, you know how to let your emotions show but you still find it difficult to do so as often as you should. You should be prepared to let your emotions out more often. When you feel sad, let yourself cry. When you feel angry, let your anger show. When you feel happy, allow a smile to cross your face. Allowing your emotions out in this way will do wonders for your physical and mental health.

If you scored 7 or less, you are definitely very uptight. You really do need to allow your emotions to hang out a little. There really isn't anything wrong in allowing people to know how you feel. The more you struggle to restrain your natural impulses, the more likely it is that those impulses will damage your health.

Do you need more excitement in your life?

Are you a victim of terminal boredom?

1. Are you in a rut? ☐
2. Do you wish that you had more responsibility? ☐
3. Do you regularly spend time—in a factory, office or at home—operating machinery or equipment over which you have no real control? ☐
4. Do you envy people who have exciting lives? ☐
5. Do you wish that there were more surprises in your life? ☐
6. Is your partner totally predictable in bed? ☐
7. Does television provide most of the highlights in your life? ☐
8. Do you usually know what you are going to do every day? ☐
9. Do you regularly suffer from boredom? ☐
10. Do you ever feel like shouting or screaming? ☐
11. Do you ever think that your life is slipping away? ☐
12. Do you ever dream of running away and finding a new life somewhere abroad? ☐
13. Are your holidays the best part of the year? ☐
14. Do you think it is true that "your schooldays are the best days of your life"? ☐
15. Do you ever feel that you are taken for granted? ☐

CHECK YOUR SCORE

1.	yes	1	no	0
2.	yes	1	no	0
3.	yes	1	no	0
4.	yes	1	no	0
5.	yes	1	no	0
6.	yes	1	no	0
7.	yes	1	no	0
8.	yes	1	no	0
9.	yes	1	no	0
10.	yes	1	no	0
11.	yes	1	no	0
12.	yes	1	no	0
13.	yes	1	no	0
14.	yes	1	no	0
15.	yes	1	no	0

Total =

If you scored 9 to 15, boredom is a big problem in your life. A widely underestimated problem, boredom is a major cause of unhappiness, depression and a wide range of other mental and physical disorders. But do not despair; it isn't difficult to balance the boredom with color and excitement. Start by looking for a rewarding pastime or hobby. Do something that you can be good at and that you can take pride in. Maybe start taking college classes. And be prepared to take risks occasionally. If you take risks and fail, then at least you'll know that you tried. If you never take risks, you'll never achieve anything. And life will remain unspeakably dull.

If you scored between 4 and 8, then although boredom isn't a major problem in your life, it can still make you feel frustrated and angry occasionally. Look back and check the questions to which you've answered yes—then try to work out *why* you've answered yes and how you can alter your lifestyle so that your attitude is healthier.

If you scored 3 or less, boredom plays only a very small part in your life. By and large you probably have all the excitement that you can handle.

How strong is your self-image?

Are you insecure? Humble? Self-effacing? Self-confident? Arrogant?

1. Once you've made a decision, do you usually have the confidence to stick with it—even if you are unpopular as a result? ☐
2. If you needed to use the lavatory at a posh dinner party, would you cross your legs and wait rather than leave the dinner table? ☐
3. If you wanted to buy sexy underwear, would you buy mail order rather than go into a shop? ☐
4. Do you think that you are a good lover? ☐
5. If you got bad service in a shop, would you have the courage to complain to the manager? ☐

6. Do you hate looking at photographs of yourself? ☐
7. Do you get very upset if people criticize you? ☐
8. Do you tend to keep your opinions to yourself? ☐
9. Do you find it difficult to believe that people are being sincere when they say nice things about you? ☐
10. Do you regularly feel inferior to people that you meet? ☐
11. Are you satisfied with your appearance? ☐
12. Do you think that you are as capable as most people of doing things? ☐
13. If you went to a party and found yourself wearing informal clothes when everyone else was dressed formally, would you be terribly embarrassed? ☐
14. Do most people like you? ☐
15. Would you describe yourself as charming? ☐
16. Do you have a good sense of humor? ☐
17. Are you good at what you do? ☐
18. Do you have good dress sense? ☐
19. Are you cool in a crisis? ☐
20. Do you work well with other people? ☐
21. Would you describe yourself as normal or average? ☐
22. Do you often wish that you looked like someone else? ☐
23. Are you frequently jealous of the accomplishments of others? ☐
24. Do you usually avoid doing things that might upset other people—even if they are things that you would like to do? ☐
25. Do you invariably dress to please others? ☐
26. Do you spend a lot of your life doing things that you don't enjoy? ☐
27. Do you let other people run your life for you? ☐

28. Do you think that you have more strengths than weaknesses? ☐
29. Do you regularly find yourself apologizing to others? ☐
30. Do you worry a lot if you accidentally upset other people? ☐
31. Do you often find yourself wishing that you had more skills and talents? ☐
32. Do you regularly need to ask others for advice? ☐
33. Do you always wait for others to break the ice at parties? ☐
34. Do you look in the mirror more than three times a day? ☐
35. Do you have a strong personality? ☐
36. Are you a good leader? ☐
37. Do you have a good memory? ☐
38. Are you attractive to members of the opposite sex? ☐
39. Are you good with money? ☐
40. Do you always ask other people for advice before buying clothes for yourself? ☐

CHECK YOUR SCORE

1.	yes	1	no	0
2.	yes	0	no	1
3.	yes	0	no	1
4.	yes	1	no	0
5.	yes	1	no	0
6.	yes	0	no	1
7.	yes	0	no	1
8.	yes	0	no	1
9.	yes	0	no	1

10.	yes	0	no	1
11.	yes	1	no	0
12.	yes	1	no	0
13.	yes	0	no	1
14.	yes	1	no	0
15.	yes	1	no	0
16.	yes	1	no	0
17.	yes	1	no	0
18.	yes	1	no	0
19.	yes	1	no	0
20.	yes	1	no	0
21.	yes	0	no	1
22.	yes	0	no	1
23.	yes	0	no	1
24.	yes	0	no	1
25.	yes	0	no	1
26.	yes	0	no	1
27.	yes	0	no	1
28.	yes	1	no	0
29.	yes	0	no	1
30.	yes	0	no	1
31.	yes	0	no	1
32.	yes	0	no	1
33.	yes	0	no	1
34.	yes	1	no	0
35.	yes	1	no	0
36.	yes	1	no	0
37.	yes	1	no	0
38.	yes	1	no	0
39.	yes	1	no	0
40.	yes	0	no	1

Total =

If you scored between 25 and 40, you have a strong self-image. You know what you are capable of and, by and large, you know your strengths as well as your weaknesses. But a word of warning: if your score gets close to 40, others could think of you as arrogant and overbearing. Perhaps, after all, you might need to temper your strength of mind with just a touch of humility.

If you scored between 12 and 24, you have a reasonably strong self-image, but you still have many doubts and feelings of insecurity. Perhaps you need to boost your self-image a little. Remind yourself of all your skills and achievements, your qualities and strengths.

If you scored 11 or less, you definitely need to give yourself a boost. You are far too humble and self-effacing, and such people often find themselves being trodden on. Try to stop thinking of your weak points—think instead of what you have to offer those around you. Concentrate on learning to respect yourself and you'll soon find that others respect you more too.

Are you frustrated?

Has your life got purpose? Do you wish that you could get more satisfaction?

1. Do you ever feel that something is lacking in your life? ☐
2. Do you have any unfulfilled ambitions? ☐
3. Do you ever feel that your life is slipping by? ☐
4. Do you wish that you had more responsibility? ☐
5. Are you proud of your achievements? ☐
6. Have you any talents that aren't fully employed? ☐
7. Are you looking forward to the future? ☐
8. Are you doing what you dreamt of when you were 18 years old? ☐
9. Are you frequently bored? ☐
10. Do you ever feel so frustrated that you could scream? ☐
11. Do other people's habits irritate you? ☐
12. Do you ever feel that you want to hit people? ☐
13. Are you rude to people who are slow or inefficient? ☐
14. Do you have lots of patience? ☐
15. Do you have a satisfying sex life? ☐

CHECK YOUR SCORE

1.	yes	1	no	0
2.	yes	1	no	0
3.	yes	1	no	0
4.	yes	1	no	0
5.	yes	0	no	1
6.	yes	1	no	0
7.	yes	0	no	1
8.	yes	0	no	1
9.	yes	1	no	0
10.	yes	1	no	0
11.	yes	1	no	0
12.	yes	1	no	0
13.	yes	1	no	0
14.	yes	0	no	1
15.	yes	0	no	1

Total =

If you scored 9 to 15, your life is full of frustrations. You need to take your life in hand—and do it now. Don't just sit there waiting for something to happen. Unless you take charge, nothing will happen and you'll remain frustrated, angry and bitter for the rest of your life. Think back a few years. What were your ambitions and dreams when you were younger? Some will no longer be practical, but many of them will still be possible. Try to realize as many as you can. Put hope and sparkle back into your life and there won't be room for frustration.

If you scored between 5 and 8, then although your life is not ruled by feelings of frustration, there are undoubtedly still times when you feel thwarted. To make sure that the problem doesn't get worse you should, perhaps, take charge of your own life a little more. Maybe you would benefit from reading the advice given above to those who scored between 9 and 15.

If you scored 4 or less, frustration does not play a large part in your life. You get your fair share of satisfaction.

How inquisitive are you?

Do you take an interest in the world around you?

1. Has anyone ever complained that you are nosy? ☐
2. Do you like visiting new places? ☐
3. Do you like meeting new people? ☐
4. Do you like being independent? ☐
5. Do you enjoy solving problems? ☐
6. Do you like knowing how things work? ☐
7. Do you enjoy documentary programs on television? ☐
8. Do you prefer biographies and non-fiction to novels? ☐
9. Have you ever tried to trace your ancestors? ☐
10. Has your curiosity ever got you into trouble? ☐

11. As a child were you ever told off for asking questions?   ☐

12. Do you like to take things apart to see how they work?   ☐

13. Do you like knowing how much other people earn?   ☐

14. Do you enjoy reading gossip items in newspapers and magazines?   ☐

15. Do you enjoy hearing gossip from friends and neighbors?   ☐

CHECK YOUR SCORE

1.	yes	1	no	0
2.	yes	1	no	0
3.	yes	1	no	0
4.	yes	1	no	0
5.	yes	1	no	0
6.	yes	1	no	0
7.	yes	1	no	0
8.	yes	1	no	0
9.	yes	1	no	0
10.	yes	1	no	0
11.	yes	1	no	0
12.	yes	1	no	0
13.	yes	1	no	0
14.	yes	1	no	0
15.	yes	1	no	0

Total =

If you scored 9 to 15, you have a strong inquisitive nature. Some people may think that you're too nosy, and others may remind you that "curiosity killed the cat." But information is one of the basic currencies of life. Keep on asking questions, remain inquisitive, continue collecting information and you'll stand a much greater chance of achieving your aims and ambitions.

If you scored 3 to 8, you have a reasonably strong inquisitive nature. Asking questions may not always endear you to others, but not asking questions will simply ensure that you don't get anywhere at all.

If you scored 2 or less, you show remarkably little interest in the world around you. If you are perfectly happy with your life as it is and you never suffer from frustration, anger or thwarted ambitions, you are probably wise to remain uninquisitive. But if you have unfulfilled ambitions or aspirations, you really need to take a greater interest in the rest of the world.

How daring are you?

Do you enjoy taking risks? Are you a daredevil or a conformist? Brave or cowardly?

1. Do you like learning new things?   □
2. Do you like unexpected guests?   □

3. Do you always prefer to go back to the same place for your holidays? ☐

4. Do you have a number of interests? ☐

5. Do you like trying out new things? ☐

6. When trying something new, do you worry a lot about looking foolish? ☐

7. Do you drive too fast? ☐

8. Do you usually catch trains, buses and airplanes at the last possible moment? ☐

9. Do you get frustrated by people who drive too slowly? ☐

10. Do you think that a few risks add spice to life? ☐

11. Do you do anything that you know is bad for your health, such as drink too much, smoke or eat animal fats? ☐

12. Have you ever signed a contract without reading the small print? ☐

13. Do you avoid dangerous rides at fairgrounds? ☐

14. If you bought a new watch, would you try smuggling it through customs to avoid paying duty/import taxes? ☐

15. Do you know which are the safest seats to choose on an airplane? ☐

16. Would you go heavily into debt to fund a business project? ☐

17. Would you prefer a safe job with good prospects and a pension to an exciting job with few prospects and no pension? ☐

18. Do you think money spent on insurance is money wasted? ☐

19. Would you find it difficult to resist a bet? ☐

20. Do you often wear daring, revealing or unusual clothes? □
21. Would you tell your boss if you thought that he was making a mistake? □
22. You meet a stranger on an airplane. He/she asks you out for a drink. Would you go? □
23. Would you go on a blind date? □
24. Would you buy a house without actually seeing it? □
25. Would you ever resign on a point of principle? □
26. Would you go to jail on a point of principle? □
27. Would you sleep in a haunted house? □
28. Would you like to make a parachute jump? □
29. Would you go bathing in the sea in winter? □
30. Would you streak for a dare? □

CHECK YOUR SCORE

1.	yes	1	no	0
2.	yes	1	no	0
3.	yes	0	no	1
4.	yes	1	no	0
5.	yes	1	no	0
6.	yes	0	no	1
7.	yes	1	no	0
8.	yes	1	no	0
9.	yes	1	no	0
10.	yes	1	no	0
11.	yes	1	no	0
12.	yes	1	no	0
13.	yes	0	no	1
14.	yes	1	no	0
15.	yes	0	no	1

16.	yes	1	no	0
17.	yes	0	no	1
18.	yes	1	no	0
19.	yes	1	no	0
20.	yes	1	no	0
21.	yes	1	no	0
22.	yes	1	no	0
23.	yes	1	no	0
24.	yes	1	no	0
25.	yes	1	no	0
26.	yes	1	no	0
27.	yes	1	no	0
28.	yes	1	no	0
29.	yes	1	no	0
30.	yes	1	no	0

Total =

If you scored between 18 and 30, you take plenty of risks—and probably often take risks without really counting the cost of failure. Risks have to be taken in order to make progress, but it is perhaps worth remembering that it is sometimes wise to balance risks with a little caution and good sense.

If you scored between 10 and 17, you take care to balance the risks in your life against the possible penalties. You are well aware of the hazards associated with certain risks and you don't hazard yourself, your possessions or those around you without first making a realistic evaluation of the outcome.

If you scored 9 or less, you are cautious and careful by nature. You don't willingly take risks and you think carefully before taking chances that could lead to disaster. Your attitude is a mature and sensible one. The disadvantage of having such a mature attitude is that life might occasionally seem a little dull and clinical.

Are you a hypochondriac?

How much do you worry about your health?

1. Do you have regular medical check-ups? ☐
2. Do you regularly buy or read medical books? ☐
3. Do you enjoy watching health programs on television? ☐
4. Do you regularly spend money on vitamins, tonics and the like? ☐
5. Do you avoid foods that you know are bad for you? ☐
6. Do you regularly spend money on home medicines? ☐
7. Do you talk a lot about your health (or lack of it)? ☐
8. If you get indigestion, do you always worry that it might be an ulcer? ☐
9. If you get a headache, do you worry that it might be a brain tumor? ☐
10. Do you often seem to suffer from mysterious ailments? ☐
11. Do you usually retire to your bed if you are upset, worried or anxious? ☐

12. Do you usually develop mild physical symptoms, such as a headache, when you are under pressure?

13. Has anyone ever accused you of malingering? ☐

14. Do you regularly have to miss important but unpleasant appointments because of ill health? ☐

15. Do you have any long-term medical problem for which your doctor has been unable to find any explanation? ☐

16. When you were small, did you ever use physical symptoms to enable you to stay away from school? ☐

17. Have you ever felt secretly pleased when you have developed an illness that has enabled you to avoid some unpleasant social event? ☐

18. When you were ill as a child, did your mother make a tremendous fuss over you? ☐

19. Do you always go straight to bed if you get a cold? ☐

20. Are other people generally unsympathetic when you are sick? ☐

21. Do you worry a lot about contracting infectious diseases? ☐

22. Do you visit your doctor more than most people you know? ☐

23. Is your medicine cabinet full of pill bottles? ☐

24. Does illness run in your family? ☐

25. Do you worry a lot about your health? ☐

26. Do you weigh yourself daily? ☐

27. Do you get lots of dizzy spells or funny turns? ☐

28. Do you suffer a lot from palpitations? ☐

29. Do you always examine the results when you have been to the lavatory? ☐

30. Do you regularly examine your tongue? ☐

CHECK YOUR SCORE

1.	yes	1	no	0
2.	yes	1	no	0
3.	yes	1	no	0
4.	yes	1	no	0
5.	yes	1	no	0
6.	yes	1	no	0
7.	yes	1	no	0
8.	yes	1	no	0
9.	yes	1	no	0
10.	yes	1	no	0
11.	yes	1	no	0
12.	yes	1	no	0
13.	yes	1	no	0
14.	yes	1	no	0
15.	yes	1	no	0
16.	yes	1	no	0
17.	yes	1	no	0
18.	yes	1	no	0
19.	yes	1	no	0
20.	yes	1	no	0
21.	yes	1	no	0
22.	yes	1	no	0
23.	yes	1	no	0
24.	yes	1	no	0
25.	yes	1	no	0
26.	yes	1	no	0
27.	yes	1	no	0
28.	yes	1	no	0
29.	yes	1	no	0
30.	yes	1	no	0

Total =

If you scored 19 to 30, you are a hypochondriac. The irony is that hypochondriacs can sometimes worry themselves into ill health. You need, perhaps, to take a healthier attitude to life. Learn to relax a little and take things as they come. Be on the look-out for early warning signs of illness, but do not allow your preoccupation with your health to dominate your life.

If you scored 6 to 18, you have a reasonably sensible attitude toward your health, but be careful not to make the mistake of allowing your concern for your health to become any more than just that. It is remarkably easy for a healthy interest to become an unhealthy state of hypochondria.

If you scored 5 or less, your attitude towards your health is sensible and well balanced.

How ambitious are you?

Are you driven by your desires, aims and yearnings?

1. Do you want to be rich and famous one day?   ☐
2. Do you think that you will be rich and famous one day?   ☐
3. Would you like a big, expensive car?   ☐

4. Do you know exactly what type of car you would like? ☐
5. Would you like to live in a big country house? ☐
6. Would you like to have servants to look after you? ☐
7. When you are playing a game, do you always like to win? ☐
8. Would you ever borrow money for a business venture? ☐
9. If you thought that you could get away with it, would you do anything dishonest? ☐
10. Would you move abroad if the prospects were better? ☐
11. Would you like to run your own business? ☐
12. Do you think that rich and famous people are, generally speaking, more interesting than other folk? ☐
13. Would you put up with hardship and penury if it meant that you would be rich one day? ☐
14. Would you like to be recognized in the street? ☐
15. Do you think that you are different to other people? ☐

CHECK YOUR SCORE

1.	yes	1	no	0
2.	yes	1	no	0
3.	yes	1	no	0
4.	yes	1	no	0
5.	yes	1	no	0
6.	yes	1	no	0
7.	yes	1	no	0
8.	yes	1	no	0
9.	yes	1	no	0
10.	yes	1	no	0

11.	yes	1	no	0
12.	yes	1	no	0
13.	yes	1	no	0
14.	yes	1	no	0
15.	yes	1	no	0

Total =

If you scored between 9 and 15, you have a strong streak of personal ambition. You are driven by powerful wants and aspirations and, given a little natural talent and a generous helping of that essential lubricant, good luck, there is no reason why you should not succeed.

If you scored between 5 and 8, you have strong ambitions but they are tempered by caution and good sense. If you really do want to succeed, you will have to throw caution to the winds and bypass good sense occasionally.

If you scored 4 or less, your personal ambitions are slight and fairly unimportant. You are happy with life the way it is and would prefer to get on with enjoying it rather than struggling for success.

How kind are you?

Are you generous and merciful or sadistic and cruel? How much do you care about others?

1. Do your friends trust you? ☐
2. Do you have friends whom you can trust? ☐
3. If your best friend rang up in trouble at 3:00 a.m., would you get up to go and help? ☐
4. Would you lend money to your best friend? ☐
5. Would you give up your weekend to help your best friend? ☐
6. Would you give up your holiday to help your best friend? ☐
7. Would you tell a good but embarrassing story about one of your friends to mutual acquaintances? ☐
8. Would you lend your favorite possessions to a friend? ☐
9. Do you usually remember your friends' birthdays? ☐
10. Would you help a stranger in trouble? ☐
11. If you were driving, would you stop to give a stranger a lift? ☐
12. Do you get upset when you see people crying? ☐
13. Do you sense people's moods and try to fit in accordingly? ☐

14. Are you genuinely delighted when friends and ac-
    quaintances enjoy good fortune?   ☐

15. Do friends often lean on you when they are in trou-
    ble?   ☐

CHECK YOUR SCORE

1.	yes	1	no	0
2.	yes	1	no	0
3.	yes	1	no	0
4.	yes	1	no	0
5.	yes	1	no	0
6.	yes	1	no	0
7.	yes	0	no	1
8.	yes	1	no	0
9.	yes	1	no	0
10.	yes	1	no	0
11.	yes	1	no	0
12.	yes	1	no	0
13.	yes	1	no	0
14.	yes	1	no	0
15.	yes	1	no	0

Total =

If you scored between 10 and 15, you are extremely generous and kindly. You suffer when others suffer and you enjoy
helping others who are less fortunate than you are. You care
a great deal about others and your caring is genuine and well
motivated.

If you scored between 5 and 9, you are a reasonably caring individual but your affection and sense of mercy towards others is not limitless.

If you scored 4 or less, you are fairly hard-hearted and not easily influenced by hard-luck stories. Friends have to learn to take you as you are: if it suits you, then you will help; but if you have other things to do, they must look after themselves.

How irascible are you?

Do you have a temper? How easily roused are you?

1. You're in a hurry and you spill milk everywhere. Would you swear? ☐

2. There is a delay at the railway station. You ask a porter for advice. He ignores you. Are you likely to snap at him? ☐

3. A waiter is rude. Would you insist on seeing the manager? ☐

4. You are waiting for a space in a car park. Someone nips in ahead of you and steals the space. Would you let the other driver know your feelings? ☐

5. Someone is rude about your physical appearance. Are you likely to get angry? ☐

6. Someone is rude about your partner or a dear friend. Are you likely to get angry? ☐

7. Someone is rude about your mother. Are you likely to get angry? ☐

8. You see someone mistreating a donkey. Would you try to stop him? ☐

9. Someone steals your place in a queue at the bank. Would you protest? ☐

10. Friends stay with you and break several items in your home. They don't apologize. Would you show your anger? ☐

11. Someone lets a door swing back into your face. Would you let him know your feelings? ☐

12. You see boys throwing stones at a cat in your garden. Would you go out and tell them off? ☐

13. A neighbor persistently arrives home late and noisily. Would you ever shout abuse? ☐

14. A relative stranger comes into your home and lights up a foul-smelling pipe or cigar. If necessary, would you insist that he either stops smoking or leaves? ☐

15. Do you ever say something in the heat of the moment and regret it afterwards? ☐

CHECK YOUR SCORE

1.	yes	1	no	0
2.	yes	1	no	0
3.	yes	1	no	0
4.	yes	1	no	0
5.	yes	1	no	0
6.	yes	1	no	0
7.	yes	1	no	0

8.	yes	1	no	0
9.	yes	1	no	0
10.	yes	1	no	0
11.	yes	1	no	0
12.	yes	1	no	0
13.	yes	1	no	0
14.	yes	1	no	0
15.	yes	1	no	0

Total =

If you scored between 10 and 15, you are easily roused. You are not the sort of individual to stand idly by and watch something happening of which you disapprove. Nor are you the sort to accept bad behavior or poor service without making your feelings known. But although your temper means that you are hard on others, you are also hard on yourself. You believe in blunt, honest, straight talking.

If you scored 5 to 9, you have a temper and can be roused into a fairly dramatic display of ire. But often you manage to control your feelings either because you dislike making a scene or because your natural sense of modesty and discretion prevails.

If you scored 4 or less, you are not easily roused. You tend to keep silent when you are angry. You nurse your grief, anger and discontent deep inside you. This isn't always wise, of course, because suppressing such emotions can, in the long run, lead to problems such as indigestion and other stress-linked disorders.

How artistic are you?

Do you have a creative nature or are you a philistine?

1. Could you write a book? ☐
2. Do you like good conversation? ☐
3. Do you prefer thinking to doing? ☐
4. Would you like to present a television program? ☐
5. Do you have difficulty in expressing yourself? ☐
6. Are you often accused of having your head in the clouds? ☐
7. Do you like unconventional people? ☐
8. Do you have lots of creative and inventive ideas? ☐
9. Do you like taking photographs? ☐
10. Do you like painting or drawing? ☐
11. Do you like looking at buildings and architecture? ☐
12. Do you design any of your own clothes? ☐
13. Do you frequently write letters to newspapers and/or magazines? ☐
14. Do you like visiting art galleries? ☐
15. Do you have good color/dress sense? ☐

CHECK YOUR SCORE

1.	yes	1	no	0
2.	yes	1	no	0
3.	yes	1	no	0
4.	yes	1	no	0
5.	yes	0	no	1
6.	yes	1	no	0
7.	yes	1	no	0
8.	yes	1	no	0
9.	yes	1	no	0
10.	yes	1	no	0
11.	yes	1	no	0
12.	yes	1	no	0
13.	yes	1	no	0
14.	yes	1	no	0
15.	yes	1	no	0

Total =

If you scored between 8 and 15, you have a strong, artistic nature. You are at your happiest when given the freedom to express yourself in some creative activity.

If you scored between 3 and 7, you have an artistic nature but creativity is not the only important part of your personality. You enjoy creating and you enjoy art (in the widest possible sense), but you would not be prepared to make sacrifices for your art. Perhaps because you enjoy the rewards of a more prosaic life?

If you scored 2 or less, you have a fairly stunted artistic nature. Occasionally you can appreciate a good piece of art, a good film or an enjoyable book. But your tastes are fairly simple. You know what you like and you have little patience with artistic pretensions.

How practical are you?

How well can you look after yourself?

1. Could you survive on a desert island? ☐
2. Can you mend a fuse? ☐
3. Can you boil an egg? ☐
4. Can you cook a three-course meal? ☐
5. Can you iron a shirt? ☐
6. Can you change a car tire? ☐
7. Do you find it easy to find solutions to practical problems? ☐
8. Are you good at mending things? ☐
9. Are you well organized? ☐
10. Could you organize an office filing system? ☐
11. Do you know how to mend a bicycle puncture? ☐
12. Could you mend a dripping tap? ☐
13. Do you know how to remove a splinter? ☐
14. Do you know how to remove a bee sting? ☐
15. Do you know how to perform artificial respiration? ☐

CHECK YOUR SCORE

1.	yes	1	no	0
2.	yes	1	no	0
3.	yes	1	no	0
4.	yes	1	no	0
5.	yes	1	no	0
6.	yes	1	no	0
7.	yes	1	no	0
8.	yes	1	no	0
9.	yes	1	no	0
10.	yes	1	no	0
11.	yes	1	no	0
12.	yes	1	no	0
13.	yes	1	no	0
14.	yes	1	no	0
15.	yes	1	no	0

Total =

If you scored between 10 and 15, you are an extremely practical individual. You can cope in difficult situations and your patience and good sense is almost inexhaustible.

If you scored between 4 and 9, you can look after yourself reasonably well. You might not be able to cope with everything with the same ease, but you can muddle through without too much difficulty.

If you scored 3 or less, you are really pretty incapable of looking after yourself. Left to your own devices you wouldn't last long. On a desert island you'd probably last a day or so.

In a big city you'd last only as long as you had enough money to hire people to do things for you.

How methodical are you?

How neat and ordered is your life?

1. Do you dislike surprises? ☐
2. Do you like well-tested solutions? ☐
3. Do people ever accuse you of being boring? ☐
4. Do you like to keep things in order? ☐
5. Do you always make a list before going shopping? ☐
6. Do you always finish what you start? ☐
7. Do you prefer machines to people? ☐
8. Do you prefer logical argument to emotional outbursts? ☐
9. Do you prefer having a deadline to work to? ☐
10. Is your home neat and tidy? ☐
11. Do you know where your passport is now? ☐
12. Have you made a will? ☐
13. Do you always pay bills on time? ☐
14. Are you usually on time for appointments? ☐
15. Do you use a diary to plan your life? ☐

CHECK YOUR SCORE

1.	yes	1	no	0
2.	yes	1	no	0
3.	yes	1	no	0
4.	yes	1	no	0
5.	yes	1	no	0
6.	yes	1	no	0
7.	yes	1	no	0
8.	yes	1	no	0
9.	yes	1	no	0
10.	yes	1	no	0
11.	yes	1	no	0
12.	yes	1	no	0
13.	yes	1	no	0
14.	yes	1	no	0
15.	yes	1	no	0

Total =

If you scored 5 or less, you are fairly disorganized! But that probably doesn't matter all that much. You almost certainly don't mind, much preferring gentle chaos to a neat and ordered life-style.

If you scored 6 to 10, you are reasonably well organized but you still get into a mess occasionally.

If you scored 11 to 15, you are extremely methodical, neat and precise in just about everything you do.

How strong is your sex drive?

Are you a sex maniac, or could you take it or leave it?

1. Do you like to have sex at least once a day? ☐
2. Could you live quite happily without ever having sex again? ☐
3. Do you only have sex when your partner feels like it? ☐
4. Do you enjoy dressing up when making love? ☐
5. Do you enjoy sexual foreplay? ☐
6. Do you enjoy experimenting with new sexual positions? ☐
7. Do you enjoy reading pornographic magazines? ☐
8. Do you enjoy watching blue movies? ☐
9. If invited to an orgy, would you go? ☐
10. Do you enjoy oral sex? ☐
11. Have you ever tried bondage/sado-masochism? ☐
12. Have you ever had sex with a stranger? ☐
13. Are you excited by the idea of having a different sexual partner every night? ☐
14. Is sex the most important pleasure in your life? ☐
15. Do you sometimes worry that you think too much about sex? ☐
16. Do you think about sex at least once a day? ☐

17. Do you find it difficult to have a platonic relationship with a member of the opposite sex? ☐

18. Are your dreams usually sexual? ☐

19. Do you normally dress to attract members of the opposite sex? ☐

20. Do you flirt a lot? ☐

21. Do you ever fantazise about having sex with friends or acquaintances? ☐

22. Do you ever fantasize about having sex with celebrities or famous people? ☐

23. Do you feel think that sex without love is unsatisfactory? ☐

24. Do you ever find yourself struggling to suppress sexual thoughts? ☐

25. Would you like to watch your partner making love to someone else? ☐

CHECK YOUR SCORE

1.	yes	1	no	0
2.	yes	0	no	1
3.	yes	0	no	1
4.	yes	1	no	0
5.	yes	1	no	0
6.	yes	1	no	0
7.	yes	1	no	0
8.	yes	1	no	0
9.	yes	1	no	0
10.	yes	1	no	0
11.	yes	1	no	0
12.	yes	1	no	0
13.	yes	1	no	0

14.	yes	1	no	0
15.	yes	1	no	0
16.	yes	1	no	0
17.	yes	1	no	0
18.	yes	1	no	0
19.	yes	1	no	0
20.	yes	1	no	0
21.	yes	1	no	0
22.	yes	1	no	0
23.	yes	0	no	1
24.	yes	1	no	0
25.	yes	1	no	0

Total =

If you scored 25, then you are a full-blooded, unashamed sex maniac.

If you scored 17 to 24, you have an extremely powerful sex drive—in fact you're not far off from being a complete sex maniac. Few things are quite as important to you as sex and other aspects of your life—business, hobbies—almost certainly take second place to your sex life.

If you scored between 5 and 16, you have a powerful sex drive that plays a dominating part in your life.

If you scored 4 or less, you manage to keep your sexual instincts and drives under some degree of control. Other things in your life are more important than mere sex.

How ruthless are you?

How strong are your scruples?

1. Would you kill to save your life? ☐
2. Would you kill to save the life of someone you love? ☐
3. Would you kill to save the life of a stranger? ☐
4. Would you kill a stranger for $1,000? ☐
5. Would you kill a stranger for $10,000? ☐
6. Would you kill a stranger for $100,000? ☐
7. Would you kill a stranger for $1,000,000? ☐
8. Would you lie to a boss to avoid a possible sacking? ☐
9. Do you value money or material gain over friendship? ☐
10. Would you risk damaging a friend's career in order to further your own? ☐
11. Would you lie to your partner to avoid a row? ☐
12. Would you lie to your parents to avoid a row? ☐
13. If you were truly starving, would you steal to eat? ☐
14. If you were offered a way of making money dishonestly—but without a risk of being caught—would you take it? ☐
15. Would you kill a stranger for $100,000,000 if you were guaranteed immunity from prosecution? ☐

CHECK YOUR SCORE

1.	yes	1	no	0
2.	yes	1	no	0
3.	yes	1	no	0
4.	yes	1	no	0
5.	yes	1	no	0
6.	yes	1	no	0
7.	yes	1	no	0
8.	yes	1	no	0
9.	yes	1	no	0
10.	yes	1	no	0
11.	yes	1	no	0
12.	yes	1	no	0
13.	yes	1	no	0
14.	yes	1	no	0
15.	yes	1	no	0

Total =

If you scored 12 to 15, you are truly ruthless. You have few scruples and would do virtually anything in order to further your own ambitions. I think it is fair to say that you normally put your personal, and particularly your financial, welfare above the welfare and health of others.

If you scored between 4 and 11, you have a strong ruthless streak, but it is tempered with caution. You do have a strong conscience.

If you scored 3 or less, you cannot be described as ruthless. Your attitude to life is dominated by a strong sense of decency and a feeling for what is right.

How much of an individual are you?

Are you independent and eccentric, or do you prefer to be one of the crowd?

1. Do you dislike routine? ☐
2. Do you like wearing daring clothes? ☐
3. Do you have an unusual career? ☐
4. Do you have a career normally associated with members of the opposite sex? ☐
5. Do you have an unusual hobby? ☐
6. Do you find "conservative" people boring? ☐
7. Do you have any unusual pets? ☐
8. Do you enjoy eating or cooking unusual food? ☐
9. Do other people make most of your decisions for you? ☐
10. Do you often find yourself in the middle of a controversy? ☐
11. Do you have a lot of will-power? ☐
12. Do you always make your own decisions—whatever others say? ☐
13. Would you describe yourself as master of your own fate? ☐
14. Do you usually like to ask for advice before making decisions? ☐

15. Do you find yourself often sticking up for unusual or unpopular causes? ☐

CHECK YOUR SCORE

1.	yes	1	no	0
2.	yes	1	no	0
3.	yes	1	no	0
4.	yes	1	no	0
5.	yes	1	no	0
6.	yes	1	no	0
7.	yes	1	no	0
8.	yes	1	no	0
9.	yes	0	no	1
10.	yes	1	no	0
11.	yes	1	no	0
12.	yes	1	no	0
13.	yes	1	no	0
14.	yes	0	no	1
15.	yes	1	no	0

Total =

If you scored 9 to 15, you are strong-minded and independent. You know your own mind and are quite prepared to put up with a certain amount of unpopularity if that is the price you have to pay for remaining independent. Some people would probably describe you as "dotty" or "eccentric." Others would describe you as merely a bit of an individual. You probably bring a lot of happiness into other people's lives since you add color to their otherwise drab existences.

If you scored between 3 and 8, you have a strong individualistic streak. You may have to conform in many areas of your life, but you are prepared to stand apart from the crowd when you think it is appropriate.

If you scored 2 or less, you probably feel embarrassed and conspicuous if you stand out from the crowd. You prefer to mingle with the masses rather than go it alone.

How content are you?

Are you satisfied with your lot or are you filled with envy?

1. Do you look at other people's clothes and think that they are better than your own? ☐
2. Do you wish you could live in a different house? ☐
3. Do you wish that you had a different job? ☐
4. When you are with one person, do you ever dream of being with someone else? ☐
5. Do you have pride in what you are doing with your life? ☐
6. Do you get on well with your partner? ☐
7. Do you get on well with your friends? ☐
8. Do you get on well with your relatives? ☐
9. Are you satisfied with your sex life? ☐
10. Are you satisfied with your physical appearance? ☐
11. Do you enjoy being alive? ☐

12. Do you often feel frustrated and angry? □
13. Do you sleep well? □
14. Do you find it fairly easy to relax? □
15. Do you feel that life has been unfair to you? □

CHECK YOUR SCORE

1.	yes	0	no	1
2.	yes	0	no	1
3.	yes	0	no	1
4.	yes	0	no	1
5.	yes	1	no	0
6.	yes	1	no	0
7.	yes	1	no	0
8.	yes	1	no	0
9.	yes	1	no	0
10.	yes	1	no	0
11.	yes	1	no	0
12.	yes	0	no	1
13.	yes	1	no	0
14.	yes	1	no	0
15.	yes	0	no	1

Total =

If you scored 9 or more, you are very content with your life. There are, inevitably, some things that you'd like to change but, by and large, you're happy with things the way they are.

If you scored between 4 and 8, you are reasonably content, although there are quite a lot of things you'd like to change if you had the chance.

If you scored 3 or less, you are undoubtedly discontent. There are many things about your world that you would like to change and few aspects of your life or life-style that you feel are really satisfying.

Are you jealous?

Is your life ruled by envy or are you satisfied with your lot?

1. Do you get angry when people you know do well? ☐
2. Do you feel that other people have an easier life? ☐
3. Are you possessive about your friends? ☐
4. Are you possessive about your belongings? ☐
5. Do you get hurt if your partner looks at photographs of former friends or lovers? ☐
6. Do you worry about your partner's previous lovers? ☐
7. Do you insist on knowing exactly what your partner is doing all the time? ☐
8. Do you get upset if other people find your partner attractive? ☐
9. Do you ever envy other people's lives? ☐
10. Do you ever envy other people's homes? ☐
11. Do you ever envy other people's clothes? ☐
12. Do you ever envy other people's sex lives? ☐
13. Do you ever envy other people's jobs? ☐

14. Do you find yourself saying bitchy things about your friends? ☐

15. Do you feel hurt if friends go out without inviting you? ☐

CHECK YOUR SCORE

1.	yes	1	no	0
2.	yes	1	no	0
3.	yes	1	no	0
4.	yes	1	no	0
5.	yes	1	no	0
6.	yes	1	no	0
7.	yes	1	no	0
8.	yes	1	no	0
9.	yes	1	no	0
10.	yes	1	no	0
11.	yes	1	no	0
12.	yes	1	no	0
13.	yes	1	no	0
14.	yes	1	no	0
15.	yes	1	no	0

Total =

If you scored 10 or more, your life truly is ruined by envy. Jealousy ruins your relationships with others and ensures that you are constantly dissatisfied with your material possessions. You really do need to try to control your jealous streak before it does permanent harm.

If you scored between 4 and 9, you have a strong jealous streak, but it is not the only emotion in your life. Jealousy affects your relationships and your feelings toward others but it does not dominate them. You would, nevertheless, benefit enormously if you could learn to conquer your feelings of envy and to appreciate those skills, relationships and material possessions to which you can claim ownership.

If you scored 3 or less, jealousy plays only a very small part in your life—and it is, after all, a fairly natural human emotion.

Are you indecisive?

Do you have difficulty in making up your mind?

1. Do you have difficulty in making decisions? ☐
2. Do you find it difficult to answer questions like these? ☐
3. Do you ever toss a coin to help you make up your mind? ☐
4. Once you have made a decision, do you ever change your mind? ☐
5. Do you worry a lot about whether or not you have made the right decision? ☐
6. Do you wish there were less choices in life? ☐
7. If you're going out, do you spend ages trying to decide what to wear? ☐

8. Do you ever get dressed, then undress and put on something entirely different? ☐
9. Do you invariably ask other people for advice when making important decisions? ☐
10. Do you lie awake worrying when you have to make important decisions? ☐
11. Do you spend hours or even weeks wondering where to go on holiday? ☐
12. In a restaurant do you find it difficult to decide what to order? ☐
13. Do you usually leave it to someone else to order the wine with a meal? ☐
14. Do small decisions give you big problems? ☐
15. When buying clothes, do you spend ages making up your mind what to choose? ☐

CHECK YOUR SCORE

1.	yes	1	no	0
2.	yes	1	no	0
3.	yes	1	no	0
4.	yes	1	no	0
5.	yes	1	no	0
6.	yes	1	no	0
7.	yes	1	no	0
8.	yes	1	no	0
9.	yes	1	no	0
10.	yes	1	no	0
11.	yes	1	no	0
12.	yes	1	no	0
13.	yes	1	no	0

| 14. | yes | 1 | no | 0 |
| 15. | yes | 1 | no | 0 |

Total =

If you scored 10 or more, you are, without any doubt, extremely indecisive. Making decisions just isn't your strong point.

If you scored between 5 and 9, sometimes you are indecisive. And sometimes you aren't . . .

If you scored 4 or less, you are normally a pretty decisive individual.

How romantic are you?

Are you in love with being in love?

1. Do you often seem to fall in love?   ☐
2. When you are in love, does your love seem to absorb all your energies and take over your entire life?   ☐
3. Do you work better when you are in love?   ☐
4. Do you think that being in love is essential for good sex?   ☐
5. Can you remember your first-ever kiss?   ☐
6. Do you believe in love at first sight?   ☐
7. Do you cry at weepy movies?   ☐

8. Do you like buying or receiving flowers? ☐
9. Would you enjoy a candelit dinner for two in a country restaurant? ☐
10. Do you carry a photo of your current partner with you? ☐
11. Do you know the color of his/her eyes? ☐
12. Can you remember the date when you first met? ☐
13. Can you remember what you were wearing? ☐
14. Can you remember what he/she was wearing? ☐
15. Do you like being in love? ☐

CHECK YOUR SCORE

1.	yes	1	no	0
2.	yes	1	no	0
3.	yes	1	no	0
4.	yes	1	no	0
5.	yes	1	no	0
6.	yes	1	no	0
7.	yes	1	no	0
8.	yes	1	no	0
9.	yes	1	no	0
10.	yes	1	no	0
11.	yes	1	no	0
12.	yes	1	no	0
13.	yes	1	no	0
14.	yes	1	no	0
15.	yes	1	no	0

Total =

If you scored 9 to 15, you are a real old-fashioned romantic. Love plays a very important part in your life.

If you scored between 4 and 8, then although love does play a part in your life, it isn't a desperately important one. You aren't one of the world's great romantics.

If you scored 3 or less, you aren't really very romantic at all. You probably buy your partner useful presents and instead of blowing money on dinner and champagne prefer to celebrate anniversaries and other occasions by buying a nest of coffee tables or a set of non-stick pans.

How sensual are you?

Are your senses well developed?

1. Do you have a favorite season? ☐
2. Do you have favorite smells? ☐
3. Do you like rainbows? ☐
4. Do you enjoy tasting new foods? ☐
5. Do you enjoy beautiful sunsets? ☐
6. Do you like being touched and massaged? ☐
7. Do you like touching people you love? ☐
8. Does music ever make you cry? ☐
9. Do smells and sounds conjure up memories for you? ☐
10. Are you aroused by perfumes? ☐
11. Do you like touching certain fabrics? ☐

12. Do you like the feel of silk on your skin? ☐
13. Do you enjoy walking on crunchy, new snow? ☐
14. Do you enjoy feeling the sun on your face? ☐
15. Do loud and intrusive noises irritate and annoy you? ☐

CHECK YOUR SCORE

1.	yes	1	no	0
2.	yes	1	no	0
3.	yes	1	no	0
4.	yes	1	no	0
5.	yes	1	no	0
6.	yes	1	no	0
7.	yes	1	no	0
8.	yes	1	no	0
9.	yes	1	no	0
10.	yes	1	no	0
11.	yes	1	no	0
12.	yes	1	no	0
13.	yes	1	no	0
14.	yes	1	no	0
15.	yes	1	no	0

Total =

If you scored between 8 and 15, you are an extremely sensual creature. Your senses are well developed and you almost certainly get great pleasure from beautiful sounds, sights and smells.

If you scored between 3 and 7, your senses are quite well developed. You have your truly sensual moments.

If you scored 2 or less, you are rather a cool individual. Nothing really seems to turn you on and you remain strangely indifferent to sensual pleasures.

How good is your memory?

How far back does it go? How reliable is it?

1. Can you remember at least five different telephone numbers? ☐
2. Do you know the number plate of the car you had five years ago? ☐
3. Do you ever completely forget appointments? ☐
4. Can you remember what you had to eat for breakfast three days ago? ☐
5. Can you remember your first kiss? ☐
6. Can you remember your first lover? ☐
7. Can you remember your first day at school? ☐
8. Can you remember a poem you learned as a child? ☐
9. Can you remember an item of clothing you had when you were 10 years old? ☐
10. Do you usually have to check telephone numbers before making calls? ☐
11. Can you remember what you were wearing when you first kissed? ☐
12. Can you remember the name of your first friend? ☐

13. Do certain smells remind you of certain places? ☐
14. Can you remember the route you used to walk, cycle or ride the bus to school when you were 12? ☐
15. Do you usually remember birthdays and anniversaries? ☐

CHECK YOUR SCORE

1.	yes	1	no	0
2.	yes	1	no	0
3.	yes	0	no	1
4.	yes	1	no	0
5.	yes	1	no	0
6.	yes	1	no	0
7.	yes	1	no	0
8.	yes	1	no	0
9.	yes	1	no	0
10.	yes	0	no	1
11.	yes	1	no	0
12.	yes	1	no	0
13.	yes	1	no	0
14.	yes	1	no	0
15.	yes	1	no	0

Total =

If you scored **11 or more,** you have an incredible memory. It goes back a long way and is probably extremely reliable.

If you scored **between 6 and 10,** you have a fairly good memory. You can remember most things quite well, though you do have the odd embarrassing lapse . . .

If you scored 5 or less, your memory is average. You probably forget important messages and appointments quite frequently. The silver lining to this particular cloud is that you've soon forgotten all but the most embarrassing incidents.

How impulsive are you?

Are you the sort of person who does things on the spur of the moment?

1. Are you easily bored by routine? ☐
2. Do you think that too much planning takes all the fun out of life? ☐
3. Do you usually make up your mind quickly? ☐
4. Do you ever act first and regret later? ☐
5. Do you buy clothes on impulse? ☐
6. Do you buy food on impulse? ☐
7. Do you ever buy things you don't really want? ☐
8. Do you ever buy clothes you never wear? ☐
9. Do you ever buy books you never read? ☐
10. Do you ever accept invitations that you later regret? ☐
11. Do you ever get yourself into a mess by acting before thinking? ☐
12. Do you make last minute holiday arrangements? ☐
13. Do you usually sleep on things before making major decisions? ☐

14. Do you have a tendency to sum people up after a first meeting? ☐
15. Do you ever organize spur-of-the-moment parties? ☐

CHECK YOUR SCORE

1.	yes	1	no	0
2.	yes	1	no	0
3.	yes	1	no	0
4.	yes	1	no	0
5.	yes	1	no	0
6.	yes	1	no	0
7.	yes	1	no	0
8.	yes	1	no	0
9.	yes	1	no	0
10.	yes	1	no	0
11.	yes	1	no	0
12.	yes	1	no	0
13.	yes	0	no	1
14.	yes	1	no	0
15.	yes	1	no	0

Total =

If you scored 10 or more, you almost certainly are the type of individual who jumps in where angels fear to tread. You have a tendency to do things first and think about them later. That means that you're often in trouble of one sort or another. On the other hand, it does mean that life is rarely dull.

If you scored between 4 and 9, you do have occasional irresistible impulses, but much of the time you manage to control your impulses.

If you scored 3 or less, you are far too sensible to submit to sudden impulses. You might feel like doing things on the spur of the moment, but you're usually far too sensible to succumb to such temptations.

How prudish are you?

What are your attitudes toward sex?

1. Do you believe that any sex act between two adults is acceptable as long as both partners are enthusiastic? ☐
2. Do you find homosexuality repulsive? ☐
3. Do you think that there is too much censorship on television? ☐
4. Would you happily watch a porno movie? ☐
5. Do you feel offended by nude photographs in magazines or newspapers? ☐
6. Would you sunbathe naked in your own garden if you were sure that no one could see you? ☐
7. Would you sunbathe naked in your own garden even if you thought that other people could see you? ☐
8. Would you be offended or embarrassed if a neighbor sunbathed naked? ☐
9. Would you go to a nudist beach? ☐
10. Have you bathed naked? ☐

11. Do you feel offended by nudity on television? ☐
12. Do you find the idea of topless waitresses offensive? ☐
13. Would you be embarrassed if a member of your family walked around the house naked? ☐
14. Would you be embarrassed if a member of your family walked around the house naked while you had a visitor? ☐
15. If you were alone in the house, would you feel embarrassed if you had to leave the bathroom or bedroom with no clothes on? ☐

CHECK YOUR SCORE

1.	yes	0	no	1
2.	yes	1	no	0
3.	yes	0	no	1
4.	yes	0	no	1
5.	yes	1	no	0
6.	yes	0	no	1
7.	yes	0	no	1
8.	yes	1	no	0
9.	yes	0	no	1
10.	yes	0	no	1
11.	yes	1	no	0
12.	yes	1	no	0
13.	yes	1	no	0
14.	yes	1	no	0
15.	yes	1	no	0
Total =				

If you scored 10 to 15, you are quite a prude. The chances are that your parents taught you that sex is something rather nasty and that exposing the human body is an extremely dirty habit that should be avoided by all decent God-fearing people. You were probably encouraged to change behind a towel when on a beach even when you were a toddler.

If you scored between 5 and 9, you have certain inhibitions—some of them quite strong—but you are nevertheless fairly broadminded.

If you scored 4 or less, you are pretty happy to accept that just about anything goes these days. You're not easily embarrassed and there isn't much that you don't approve of.

How thrifty are you?

Are you a Scrooge or a spendaholic?

1. Do you manage your money well? ☐
2. Do you always know how much money you have in the bank? ☐
3. Do you keep a careful check on your debts? ☐
4. Do you ever leave lights burning in unoccupied rooms? ☐
5. Do you ever throw away tubes of toothpaste that aren't quite empty? ☐

6. Do you always shop carefully—and look for bargains? ☐

7. If you buy clothes you don't like, do you still wear them until they wear out? ☐

8. If you buy food you don't like, do you eat it anyway rather than throw it away? ☐

9. When you spot a bargain, do you always buy as much as you can afford? ☐

10. Do you ever buy things that are cheap even if you don't really want them? ☐

11. Do you forget to pay bills and incur high interest charges? ☐

12. Do you ever buy things that you don't really want? ☐

13. Do you feel comfortable only when you have money saved for a "rainy day"? ☐

14. Are you, or have you ever been, seriously in debt? ☐

15. Are you a generous giver to causes you approve of? ☐

CHECK YOUR SCORE

1.	yes	1	no	0
2.	yes	1	no	0
3.	yes	1	no	0
4.	yes	0	no	1
5.	yes	0	no	1
6.	yes	1	no	0
7.	yes	1	no	0
8.	yes	1	no	0
9.	yes	1	no	0
10.	yes	0	no	1
11.	yes	0	no	1

12.	yes	0	no	1
13.	yes	1	no	0
14.	yes	0	no	1
15.	yes	0	no	1

Total =

If you scored 11 to 15, you are careful and sensible with money. You spend and buy wisely, and rarely have any real money problems. (Though you may well have had money problems in the past!)

If you scored between 5 and 10, you try hard to look after money but somehow it often seems to slip through your fingers.

If you scored 4 or less, you're really not very good with money. In fact that is probably a gross understatement; you're probably pretty bad with money. You either spend it, give it away or simply squander it.

How tolerant are you?

How strong—and how numerous—are your prejudices?

1. Would you object if someone wanted to open a sex shop near your home? ☐

2. Would you object if someone wanted to open a hospital for mental patients near your home? ☐

3. Would you object if someone wanted to open a half-way house for prisoners near your home? ☐

4. Would you object if a new religious cult wanted to open its headquarters near your home? ☐

5. Do you think that lower moral standards are responsible for many of the problems in our society? ☐

6. Would you be desperately upset if you found out that your son is a homosexual? ☐

7. Would you be desperately upset if you found out that your daughter is a lesbian? ☐

8. If your son wanted to live with a much older woman, would you be happy about it? ☐

9. If your daughter wanted to live with a much older man, would you be happy about it? ☐

10. Do you listen to speeches and broadcasts made by politicians belonging to parties that you do not support? ☐

11. Do you think that women should be allowed to become priests in the Catholic church? ☐

12. Do you think that any one race is superior to any other? ☐

13. Do you judge people by the clothes they wear? ☐

14. Do you think that women and men should always be treated equally? ☐

15. Do you get angry if people do not agree with your political or religious views? ☐

CHECK YOUR SCORE

1.	yes	1	no	0
2.	yes	1	no	0
3.	yes	1	no	0
4.	yes	1	no	0
5.	yes	1	no	0
6.	yes	1	no	0
7.	yes	1	no	0
8.	yes	0	no	1
9.	yes	0	no	1
10.	yes	0	no	1
11.	yes	0	no	1
12.	yes	1	no	0
13.	yes	1	no	0
14.	yes	0	no	1
15.	yes	1	no	0

Total =

If you scored 10 or more, you are low on tolerance and high on prejudice.

If you scored between 4 and 9, you try hard to be fair, but you have a number of strong prejudices, which you have great difficulty in suppressing.

If you scored 3 or less, you are low on prejudice and high on tolerance. But even you probably have a few "weak points" and a few half-hidden prejudices bubbling away just beneath the surface of your mind.

How vain are you?

How much is your life influenced by personal vanity?

1. Do you often stop and look at your reflection in shop windows? ☐
2. Have you ever had cosmetic surgery? ☐
3. Have you ever contemplated cosmetic surgery? ☐
4. Do you regularly spend time or money looking after your nails? ☐
5. Do you like looking at photographs of yourself? ☐
6. Do you try to get a good sun-tan before going on holiday? ☐
7. Do you try to wear clothes that enhance your looks? ☐
8. Do you brush or comb your hair more than three times a day? ☐
9. Do you have a car with personalized number plates? ☐
10. Would you pay more for luggage that carried a designer label? ☐
11. Would you pay more for clothes with a designer label? ☐
12. Do you get embarrassed by scruffy friends? ☐
13. Would you like to have a title of some sort? ☐

14. Do you spend more than you can really afford on maintaining your looks and appearance? ☐
15. Do you enjoy being photographed? ☐

CHECK YOUR SCORE

1.	yes	1	no	0
2.	yes	1	no	0
3.	yes	1	no	0
4.	yes	1	no	0
5.	yes	1	no	0
6.	yes	1	no	0
7.	yes	1	no	0
8.	yes	1	no	0
9.	yes	1	no	0
10.	yes	1	no	0
11.	yes	1	no	0
12.	yes	1	no	0
13.	yes	1	no	0
14.	yes	1	no	0
15.	yes	1	no	0

Total =

If you scored between 10 and 15, you are undoubtedly and undeniably vain. You take great pride in your personal appearance and you probably enjoy looking smart and well groomed. You like to look your best and see absolutely nothing wrong in that—and why should you?

If you scored 4 to 9, you have a few quite powerful vanities but you don't really fit into the genuinely vain category. Perhaps you're a little bit laid-back about your appearance and your image. Or perhaps you just feel that there are other things in life that are more important.

If you scored 3 or less, vanity is not one of your vices. You make the occasional effort to look presentable but you can't see the point in spending hours and hours honing your appearance. Other, more vain individuals may consider you scruffy or untidy. You prefer to think of yourself as above such considerations and more concerned with ethereal qualities than with earthly appearances.

How stubborn are you?

Are you obstinate, tenacious and stubborn?

1. If you were trying to make a telephone call and you got cut off four times, would you give up? ☐
2. You want to buy plain black shoes. You've tried eight shoe shops without success. It is raining. There is still one shop on the far side of town. Would you accept the "nearly" plain black shoes that are in front of you? ☐
3. Do you always like to have the last word in an argument? ☐
4. Do people find your opinions difficult to shake? ☐
5. Have you ever been described as pigheaded? ☐

6. If you wanted to go out with someone but got turned down, would you try again and again? ☐

7. If there was a queue for a restaurant table, would you go somewhere else? ☐

8. You spend hours making something but right at the end it goes wrong. Would you start again? ☐

9. If you failed your driving test, would you keep on taking it indefinitely until you passed? ☐

10. If there was a queue for a theater or cinema, would you go somewhere else? ☐

11. Do you have the patience to spend a day trying to repair something? ☐

12. Do you like jigsaw puzzles? ☐

13. Do you like crossword puzzles? ☐

14. Do you have the patience to practice enough to become a golf or tennis star? ☐

15 Do you lose your temper easily? ☐

CHECK YOUR SCORE

1.	yes	0	no	1
2.	yes	0	no	1
3.	yes	1	no	0
4.	yes	1	no	0
5.	yes	1	no	0
6.	yes	1	no	0
7.	yes	0	no	1
8.	yes	1	no	0
9.	yes	1	no	0
10.	yes	0	no	1
11.	yes	1	no	0
12.	yes	1	no	0

13.	yes	1	no	0
14.	yes	1	no	0
15.	yes	0	no	1

Total =

If you scored 10 to 15, you are obstinate and stubborn but probably pretty patient too. Once you've made up your mind about something, you are difficult to budge. Even when there are lots of easier (and possibly cheaper) options, you remain pigheaded and determined.

If you scored between 5 and 9, you are able to balance your obstinacy with the occasional compromise. You recognize that you can't always get your own way and that the easy way out doesn't necessarily mean lowering your personal standards.

If you scored 4 or less, you are usually quick to find the easiest, most painless solution to any problem. You don't have much patience and no one could describe you as stubborn.

Are you a snob?

Are you easygoing and easy on your friends, or do you have high expectations?

1. Do you peek at labels on other people's clothes and luggage? □

2. If you were working around the house in old clothes and you had to go into town to buy something, would you get changed? □

3. Do you feel happy and comfortable if you mix with people who are poorer than you are? □

4. If you go out to dinner, do you always choose dishes that you know how to tackle, avoiding exotic things in case you end up looking silly? □

5. If a friend called for you in an old, rusty motor car, would you be embarrassed? □

6. Do you throw out clothes, even if they are comfortable, if they look worn, frayed or out of fashion? □

7. Do you ever feel ashamed of your accent? □

8. Do you keep one set of clothes for best? □

9. Do you ever feel ashamed of your background? □

10. Do you wish that you'd been given a better education? □

11. Do you always prefer to travel first class? ☐
12. Do you put on a different, slightly posher voice when you answer the telephone? ☐
13. Do you enjoy meeting famous, rich or important people? ☐
14. Would you like to be driven everywhere in a limousine? ☐
15. Do you ever lie about your background, your parents or your wealth? ☐

CHECK YOUR SCORE

1.	yes	1	no	0
2.	yes	1	no	0
3.	yes	0	no	1
4.	yes	1	no	0
5.	yes	1	no	0
6.	yes	1	no	0
7.	yes	1	no	0
8.	yes	1	no	0
9.	yes	1	no	0
10.	yes	1	no	0
11.	yes	1	no	0
12.	yes	1	no	0
13.	yes	1	no	0
14.	yes	1	no	0
15.	yes	1	no	0

Total =

If you scored between 8 and 15, you are undoubtedly and undeniably a snob. Sadly, you allow your social aspirations to influence your attitudes to others. And your attempts to match up to your own high standards inevitably mean that you are constantly under a great deal of unnecessary pressure.

If you scored between 3 and 7, you have a strong snobbish streak, but it is under control most of the time.

If you scored 2 or less, you probably feel comfortable in any surroundings and with any people from any social background. Ironically, perhaps, your lack of social consciousness probably means that you are remarkably capable of mixing with people who are your social superiors.

How honorable are you?

Are you honest or are you not quite so honest?

1. If you saw $10 fall out of an armored security van, and knew no one would see you take it, would you chase after the van to give back the money? ☐
2. What about $1,000? Again, no one would see if you kept the money—and it belongs to a bank, not an individual. ☐
3. What about $100,000? ☐

4. What about $1,000,000? (Assume for the sake of argument that you could pick up $1,000,000 worth of currency.) ☐

5. Have you ever given the impression that you are richer than you are? ☐

6. Someone at work is stealing from the boss. Would you tell? ☐

7. Have you ever stolen anything from a shop? ☐

8. If you were driving and bumped into an empty, stationary car, would you leave a note with your name and address? ☐

9. Have you ever ''forgotten'' to include something on your tax return? ☐

10. If you broke something in a friend's house, would you tell him or her, even if there was an excellent chance they wouldn't find out that you had done it? ☐

11. If you were undercharged in a shop, would you tell the cashier? ☐

12. If a waiter in a restaurant forgot to include your wine on the bill, would you tell him? ☐

13. Have you ever feigned illness to get time off work? ☐

14. Would you be prepared to bribe someone in order to make money for your company? ☐

15. Would you be prepared to bribe someone in order to make money for yourself? ☐

CHECK YOUR SCORE

1.	yes	1	no	0
2.	yes	1	no	0
3.	yes	1	no	0
4.	yes	1	no	0

5.	yes	0	no	1
6.	yes	1	no	0
7.	yes	0	no	1
8.	yes	1	no	0
9.	yes	0	no	1
10.	yes	1	no	0
11.	yes	1	no	0
12.	yes	1	no	0
13.	yes	0	no	1
14.	yes	0	no	1
15.	yes	0	no	1

Total =

If you scored 10 or more, you are extremely honest and honorable. You can look yourself full in the face in the mirror every morning without flinching.

If you scored between 4 and 9, you are basically honest and fairly honorable. However, you can be persuaded away from the straight and narrow—particularly if you think that you are unlikely to be caught.

If you scored 3 or less, you have a flexible attitude toward the truth and a malleable conscience. I am, however, impressed that you answered the questions in this quiz so honestly.

How good is your sense of humor?

Do you let enough laughter into your life?

1. Do you find it difficult to laugh at yourself? ☐
2. Do you get cross if other people laugh at you? ☐
3. Do you like funny films? ☐
4. Do you like amusing books? ☐
5. Do you get cross if you are in an important meeting and someone starts to tell a joke or a funny story? ☐
6. Would you be deeply offended if you did something silly and people laughed at you? ☐
7. Do you think that practical jokes are childish? ☐
8. Do you think that people who laugh a lot are immature? ☐
9. Would you be embarrassed to laugh out loud in a hospital or church? ☐
10. Do you prefer serious documentaries to comedies on TV? ☐
11. Do you think that your position or status means that you need to behave in a serious way in public? ☐
12. Can you remember when you last had a really good laugh? ☐
13. Do you ever laugh out loud when you are by yourself? ☐

14. Would you be embarrassed if a line in a good book
    made you laugh?   ☐
15. Do you find quite a lot of modern humor offensive? ☐

CHECK YOUR SCORE

1.	yes	0	no	1
2.	yes	0	no	1
3.	yes	1	no	0
4.	yes	1	no	0
5.	yes	0	no	1
6.	yes	0	no	1
7.	yes	0	no	1
8.	yes	0	no	1
9.	yes	0	no	1
10.	yes	0	no	1
11.	yes	0	no	1
12.	yes	1	no	0
13.	yes	1	no	0
14.	yes	0	no	1
15.	yes	0	no	1

Total =

If you scored 11 to 15, you have a strong sense of humor.
Most important of all, perhaps, is the fact that you don't take
yourself too seriously.

If you scored between 5 and 10, you have a good sense of
humor, but you do hold yourself back occasionally. Perhaps
you do this because you feel guilty about enjoying yourself
or perhaps because you think that you ought to behave with

decorum. Learn to let yourself go a little more and you'll benefit enormously.

If you scored 4 or less, you really do need to learn to let yourself go. Learning to laugh will improve your health and enhance your relationships with others.

How trusting are you?

Are you the suspicious type?

1. Do you think that people talk about you behind your back? ☐
2. Do you believe that every man has his price? ☐
3. Do you suspect that most people cheat on their taxes? ☐
4. Do you suspect that most people would be unfaithful if they could get away with it? ☐
5. Do you have difficulty trusting people? ☐
6. Do you dislike lending things because you suspect that people won't look after them properly? ☐
7. Would you go out and leave workmen in your home? ☐
8. Do you always check your bank statements? ☐
9. Do you always check your change in shops? ☐

10. Do you take care never to leave anything of value lying around? ☐

11. Do you believe that most people would cheat you if they had the chance? ☐

12. If something is missing, do you automatically assume that it has been stolen? ☐

13. If you need directions or advice when traveling, do you usually ask at least two people the same question? ☐

14. If someone cancels an appointment, do you usually assume that they have an ulterior motive? ☐

15. Do you think that most people are basically honest? ☐

CHECK YOUR SCORE

1.	yes	0	no	1
2.	yes	0	no	1
3.	yes	0	no	1
4.	yes	0	no	1
5.	yes	0	no	1
6.	yes	0	no	1
7.	yes	1	no	0
8.	yes	0	no	1
9.	yes	0	no	1
10.	yes	0	no	1
11.	yes	0	no	1
12.	yes	0	no	1
13.	yes	0	no	1
14.	yes	0	no	1
15.	yes	1	no	0

Total =

If you scored 10 to 15, you are extremely trusting. You believe that most people are basically honest and reliable. You will, almost inevitably, be disappointed from time to time. Some people will take advantage of your trusting nature, others will simply let you down. But enjoying a suspicion-free world is probably well worth that small price.

If you scored between 5 and 9, you probably *want* to trust people. However, experience has taught you that there are many dishonest folk around, so you temper your trust with a little scepticism.

If you scored 4 or less, you are definitely low on trust and high on suspicion. It is, perhaps, worth remembering that such a complete lack of trust is only a whisper away from paranoia.

Are you a workaholic?

Are you lazy or do you push yourself too hard?

1. Do you regularly spend evenings working? ☐
2. Do you regularly spend weekends working? ☐
3. Do you have difficulty in sitting still doing nothing? ☐
4. Do you feel guilty if you stay in bed on Sunday mornings? ☐

5. Are you kept awake at night by worries about work? ☐
6. Do you dislike holidays? ☐
7. Do you normally get up very early in the morning? ☐
8. Do you have few interests outside your work? ☐
9. Do your relatives complain that you spend too much time working? ☐
10. Do your friends complain that they see little of you? ☐
11. Do you find it difficult to slow down or reduce your workload? ☐
12. Do you ever wish that your parents had shown you more love and affection? ☐
13. Do you ever work while you are eating? ☐
14. Do you get edgy and restless if you have nothing to do? ☐
15. Do you ever wake up at night and work on problems? ☐

CHECK YOUR SCORE

1.	yes	1	no	0
2.	yes	1	no	0
3.	yes	1	no	0
4.	yes	1	no	0
5.	yes	1	no	0
6.	yes	1	no	0
7.	yes	1	no	0
8.	yes	1	no	0
9.	yes	1	no	0
10.	yes	1	no	0
11.	yes	1	no	0
12.	yes	1	no	0
13.	yes	1	no	0

14.	yes	1	no	0
15.	yes	1	no	0

Total =

If you scored 3 or more, you are undeniably a workaholic, and your attitude toward work is very probably damaging your health and your relationships with your family and friends. Most workaholics push themselves constantly because as children they were denied praise and affection by their parents. Even success is no antidote to this condition; many workaholics are rich and powerful and yet unable to slow themselves down. It takes real effort for the genuine workaholic to slow down a little and allow himself more time to relax. Having said all that, it is also important to point out that workaholics do often tend to become extremely successful at what they do. If they work for large corporations, they often rise to the top. If they run their own companies, those companies often do very well indeed.

If you scored 2 or less, your attitude toward work is a healthy one. You may well enjoy what you do for a living, but you enjoy others things too and you are not prepared to allow your work to dominate your life. The only snag is that your laid-back attitude toward work means that you are relatively unlikely to reach the top.

Have you got your priorities right?

Are you driven by superficial wants rather than by basic needs?

1. Do you spend enough time doing things that you enjoy most? ☐
2. Do you spend too much time doing things you dislike? ☐
3. Do you have enough fun in your life? ☐
4. Do you find it easy to delegate responsibility? ☐
5. Do you always make sure that the important things in your life take precedence? ☐
6. Do you spend too much time earning money to buy possessions you don't really need? ☐
7. Do you spend enough time enjoying yourself? ☐
8. Do you regularly spend time with people whom you dislike? ☐
9. Do you ever think that you are wasting too much of your life? ☐
10. Do you spend enough time with your family? ☐
11. Do you spend enough time with your friends? ☐
12. Do you spend enough time on your hobbies and interests? ☐
13. Do you own more than two overcoats? ☐

14. Do you own more than six pairs of shoes?   ☐
15. Do you spend a lot of time doing boring, unsatis-
    fying things?   ☐

CHECK YOUR SCORE

1.	yes	1	no	0
2.	yes	0	no	1
3.	yes	1	no	0
4.	yes	1	no	0
5.	yes	1	no	0
6.	yes	0	no	1
7.	yes	1	no	0
8.	yes	0	no	1
9.	yes	0	no	1
10.	yes	1	no	0
11.	yes	1	no	0
12.	yes	1	no	0
13.	yes	0	no	1
14.	yes	0	no	1
15.	yes	0	no	1

Total =

If you scored 9 or more, you have got your priorities sorted out properly. You are careful to put the important things in your life first and you are wise enough to be able to put friendship, love, laughter and happiness above mere material success.

If you scored between 4 and 8, you are having a struggle to get your priorities right. You try hard to spend time on the things that mean most to you, but somehow you often seem to get seduced back into the maelstrom of twentieth-century living. You spend too much time doing things you don't like with people you don't like in order to earn money to buy possessions that you don't really need. Your priority is, perhaps, to get your needs and your wants into perspective.

If you scored 3 or less, your life is, to put it bluntly, in a mess. You spend far too much time doing things you hate and you spend far too little time doing things you enjoy with people that you like. You need to sort out your priorities. What do you really want out of life? How can you best go about satisfying those aims?

Are you liberated?

Or are you a sexist?

1. Do you think that women should do most of the household chores? ☐
2. Do you think that women should stay at home until the children have grown up? ☐
3. Do you think that men are emotionally stronger than women? ☐
4. Do you think that a woman should choose her clothes with her man in mind? ☐

5. If a woman earns more than a man, do you think she should keep quiet about it? ☐

6. Do you think it is wrong for a woman to make a pass at a man? ☐

7. Do you think that men make better car drivers than women? ☐

8. Do you think that men should always make the first move in bed? ☐

9. If both parents go out to work and their child is ill, do you think it should always be the woman who has time off work? ☐

10. Do you think it is true that women are the weaker sex? ☐

11. Do you think that women should get equal pay for doing the same work as men? ☐

12. Do you think that men should stand up for women and open the doors for them when going in and out of rooms? ☐

13. Do you think that men should help with household chores and shopping? ☐

14. Do you think that women make good surgeons and barristers? ☐

15. Do you think that women make better politicians than men? ☐

16. Do you think that women make better doctors than men? ☐

17. Do you think that women make better nurses than men? ☐

18. Do you think that men are better than women at organizing things? ☐

19. Do you think that women make better drivers than men? ☐

20. Do you think that women are more tactful than men? ☐
21. Do you think that men are better than women at cooking? ☐
22. Do you think that women are more caring than men? ☐
23. Do you think that women are usually more generous than men? ☐
24. Do you think that women are better with children than men? ☐
25. Do you think that women are more creative than men? ☐

CHECK YOUR SCORE

1.	yes	1	no	0
2.	yes	1	no	0
3.	yes	1	no	0
4.	yes	1	no	0
5.	yes	1	no	0
6.	yes	1	no	0
7.	yes	1	no	0
8.	yes	1	no	0
9.	yes	1	no	0
10.	yes	1	no	0
11.	yes	0	no	1
12.	yes	1	no	0
13.	yes	0	no	1
14.	yes	0	no	1
15.	yes	1	no	0
16.	yes	1	no	0
17.	yes	1	no	0

18.	yes	1	no	0
19.	yes	1	no	0
20.	yes	1	no	0
21.	yes	1	no	0
22.	yes	1	no	0
23.	yes	1	no	0
24.	yes	1	no	0
25.	yes	1	no	0

Total =

If you scored even 1 in this quiz, you are a sexist. If you scored 3 or more, your sexism is probably offensive to others. You need to look hard at your attitudes and prejudices. Incidentally, although many of the questions in this quiz tested for traditional male superiority sexism, some of the questions tested for female superiority sexism. Both types can be disruptive and offensive.

Are you a positive or a negative thinker?

Are you the sort of person who usually sees the black side of things?

1. Are you as happy as anyone you know? ☐
2. Do you ever wake up in the morning feeling on top of the world? ☐

3. Do you feel that other people get all the lucky breaks? □
4. Do you seem to get more than your fair share of bad luck? □
5. Do you ever feel miserable for no very good reason? □
6. Do things often seem hopeless to you? □
7. Do you frequently feel that your life is pointless? □
8. Do you think that the world is basically a miserable place? □
9. Does noise irritate you a lot? □
10. Do you feel that you get a raw deal out of life? □
11. Do you smile as much as most people you know? □
12. Do you laugh as much as most people? □
13. Do you often feel tired and listless for no very good reason? □
14. Do you think that your life has been spoiled by other people? □
15. Do you find that setbacks worry and upset you a lot? □

CHECK YOUR SCORE

1.	yes	0	no	1
2.	yes	0	no	1
3.	yes	1	no	0
4.	yes	1	no	0
5.	yes	1	no	0
6.	yes	1	no	0
7.	yes	1	no	0
8.	yes	1	no	0
9.	yes	1	no	0

10.	yes	1	no	0
11.	yes	0	no	1
12.	yes	0	no	1
13.	yes	1	no	0
14.	yes	1	no	0
15.	yes	1	no	0

Total =

If you scored 8 or more, your life is dominated by your negative attitudes. You may well have had a lot of bad breaks, but your attitude undoubtedly makes things far worse. Your "negative waves" don't just have an adverse influence on your approach to life, they also have an adverse influence on the attitudes of others.

If you scored 3 to 7, you try to be positive, but you aren't always successful. Your emotional outlook is often gloomy—and the consequence may well be that your gloom merely breeds more gloom.

If you scored 2 or less, you have a fairly healthy, positive outlook. You believe that it is important to try to remain cheerful whatever is happening and however much fate seems to be opposing you. Your positive attitude will, in the long run, help you thrive.

Your Know Yourself
SCORESHEET

QUIZ	SCORE
How optimistic are you?	. . . . .
How much of a worrier are you?	. . . . .
How sociable are you?	. . . . .
How obsessive are you?	. . . . .
How absent-minded are you?	. . . . .
How assertive are you?	. . . . .
How responsible are you?	. . . . .
How dominating are you?	. . . . .
Are you a doer or a thinker?	. . . . .
How loyal are you?	. . . . .
How intuitive are you?	. . . . .
How imaginative are you?	. . . . .
How vulnerable are you to guilty feelings?	. . . . .
How emotional are you?	. . . . .
Do you need more excitement in your life?	. . . . .
How strong is your self-image?	. . . . .
Are you frustrated?	. . . . .
How inquisitive are you?	. . . . .
How daring are you?	. . . . .
Are you a hypochondriac?	. . . . .
How ambitious are you?	. . . . .

How kind are you?   . . . . .
How irascible are you?   . . . . .
How artistic are you?   . . . . .
How practical are you?   . . . . .
How methodical are you?   . . . . .
How strong is your sex drive?   . . . . .
How ruthless are you?   . . . . .
How much of an individual are you?   . . . . .
How content are you?   . . . . .
Are you jealous?   . . . . .
Are you indecisive?   . . . . .
How romantic are you?   . . . . .
How sensual are you?   . . . . .
How good is your memory?   . . . . .
How impulsive are you?   . . . . .
How prudish are you?   . . . . .
How thrifty are you?   . . . . .
How tolerant are you?   . . . . .
How vain are you?   . . . . .
How stubborn are you?   . . . . .
Are you a snob?   . . . . .
How honorable are you?   . . . . .
How good is your sense of humor?   . . . . .
How trusting are you?   . . . . .
Are you a workaholic?   . . . . .
Have you got your priorities right?   . . . . .
Are you liberated?   . . . . .
Are you a positive or a negative thinker?   . . . . .

PART TWO

Are you an extrovert or an introvert?

Add together your scores from the following questionnaires:

How sociable are you?	. . . . .
Are you a doer or a thinker?	. . . . .
How emotional are you?	. . . . .
How daring are you?	. . . . .
How practical are you?	. . . . .
How impulsive are you?	. . . . .
Total	. . . . .

If you scored between 90 and 135, you are definitely an extrovert.

If you scored between 41 and 89, you are neither a confirmed extrovert nor a confirmed introvert. Your moods and nature change very much according to circumstances.

If you scored 40 or less, you are definitely an introvert.

How stable are you?

Begin by giving yourself 200 points.

Now add together your scores from the following questionnaires:

How obsessive are you? . . . .
How emotional are you? . . .
How strong is your self-image? . .
How much of an individual are you?
How content are you? . .
How good is your sense of humor? .
Have you got your priorities right?
Subtotal 1 . .
Plus starter points . 200
Subtotal 2 .
Next, add your scores from the following questionnaires:
How much of a worrier are you? . . . .
How vulnerable are you to guilty feelings? . . .
Are you frustrated? .
Are you a hypochondriac? . .
Are you a positive or a negative thinker? . .
Subtotal 3 .

To obtain your final score subtract Subtotal 3 from Subtotal 2.

Total   . . . . .

If you scored between 250 and 360, you are extremely stable, and an unlikely candidate for a nervous breakdown!

If you scored between 162 and 249, you are reasonably tough but you do have a number of vulnerable points. You could, perhaps, improve your mental fitness by following some of the advice in this book. To check out your weak points refer back to the first part of this book and see where your scores were weakest.

If you scored between 80 and 161, you really are very vulnerable. You need to work hard to improve your mental fitness. Check out your weak points by referring back to the first part of this book.

How vulnerable to stress are you?

Begin by giving yourself 200 points.

Now add together your scores from the following questionnaires:

How much of a worrier are you? . .

How vulnerable are you to guilty feelings? .

Are you frustrated? . .

Are you a hypochondriac? . . .

How vain are you? . . .

Are you a positive or negative thinker? . . .

Subtotal 1 . . .

Plus starter points . 200

Subtotal 2 . . .

Next, add together your scores from the following questionnaires:

How optimistic are you? . . . .

How obsessive are you? .

How emotional are you? . .

How strong is your self-image? . . .

How content are you? . . .

How good is your sense of humor? . . . .

Have you got your priorities right?

Subtotal 3 . . . .

To find out if you are vulnerable to stress subtract Subtotal 3 from Subtotal 2.

Total . .

If you scored between 228 and 335, you are extremely vulnerable to stress. There is a real chance that your physical or mental health could be adversely affected. Try to reduce your susceptibility and enhance your resistance to stress by learning how to relax both your mind and your body. Reduce your exposure to unnecessary stress by cutting down on your commitments as much as possible.

If you scored between 120 and 227, you are moderately susceptible to stress. You can reduce your susceptibility still further by learning how to relax both your body and your mind. You can also help yourself by cutting down your commitments and reducing your exposure to unnecessary stress and pressure.

If you scored 119 or less, your resistance to stress is already high. You are unlikely to suffer from any of the physical or mental problems associated with exposure to stress.

Are you the sort of stuff of which heroes are made?

Begin by giving yourself 20 points.

Now add together your scores from the following questionnaires:

Are you a doer or a thinker?	. . . .
How daring are you?	. . .
How kind are you?	. .
How much of an individual are you?	. . .
How impulsive are you?	. .
Subtotal 1	. .
Plus starter points	. 20
Subtotal 2	

Next, record your score from the following questionnaire:

Are you indecisive?   . . . . .

This is Subtotal 3

To find out if you are the sort of stuff of which heroes are made subtract Subtotal 3 from Subtotal 2.

Total   . . . . .

If you scored between 75 and 115, you are real potential hero material! If you haven't already won a medal, there is an excellent chance that one day you will.

If you scored between 37 and 74, then, although you may never think of yourself as a hero, you might just surprise yourself.

If you scored 36 or less, your cautiousness and strongly developed sense of self-preservation means that you are unlikely ever to be a hero. But who knows? Heroes *can* be made from the most unlikely materials.

How charming are you?

Begin by giving yourself 100 points.

Now add together your scores from the following questionnaires:

How sociable are you?

How loyal are you?

How emotional are you?

How kind are you?

How content are you?

How stubborn are you?

How honorable are you?

How good is your sense of humor?

How trusting are you?

Subtotal 1

Plus starter points   100

Subtotal 2

Next, add together your scores from the following questionnaires:

How irascible are you?

How ruthless are you?

Are you jealous?

How tolerant are you?

Are you liberated?

Are you a positive or a negative thinker?

Subtotal 3

To find out how charming you are subtract Subtotal 3 from Subtotal 2.

Total

If you scored between 190 and 265, you are incredibly charming. A real "prince" or "princess" charming, equally at ease among friends and strangers. You are endlessly patient and loving.

If you scored between 91 and 189, you are extremely charming but you do have your limitations. With people who are boorish, unkind, ungenerous, rude, aggressive or in any way unpleasant, you can turn off the charm!

If you scored 90 or less, your charm is restricted to those whom you love and care for. Strangers have to earn your respect and you don't worry about exposing your prejudices and personal feelings in the company of others.

How good a friend are you?

Begin by giving yourself 100 points.

Now add together your scores from the following question-naires:

How sociable are you? . . . . .
How loyal are you? . . . . .
How kind are you? . . . . .
How honorable are you? . . . . .
How good is your sense of humor? . . . . .
How trusting are you? . . . . .
Subtotal 1 . . . . .
Plus starter points . 100 .
Subtotal 2 . . . . .

Next, add together your scores from the following question-naires:

Are you jealous? . . .
How tolerant are you? . . . .
Are you a snob? . . . .
Subtotal 3 . . .
To find out how good a friend you are subtract
Subtotal 3 from Subtotal 2.
Total . . . .

If you scored over 160, you are a truly marvelous friend, reliable, loving, trusting, loyal and good-humored. In fact, it is probably no exaggeration to say that you frequently put your friends first and yourself last.

If you scored between 120 and 159, you are an excellent friend, kind, loyal and honorable. You are, however, a little wary of others and it takes some time before you give your friends your whole-hearted trust and affection. But once committed to a relationship your friendship is unshakeable.

If you scored 119 or less, you are wary of others and reluctant to commit yourself whole-heartedly to friendships. You have, perhaps, been taken advantage of in the past, or maybe people have let you down.

What sort of job is right for you?

First, complete the following five Career Guidance Clinics.

CAREER GUIDANCE CLINIC 1

Add up your scores from the following questionnaires:

How sociable are you?	. . . . .
How kind are you?	. . . . .
How stubborn are you?	. . . . .
How trusting are you?	. . . . .
Total	. . . . .

CAREER GUIDANCE CLINIC 2

Begin by giving yourself 100 points.

Now, add up your scores from the following questionnaires:

How assertive are you?	. . . . .
How practical are you?	. . . . .
How methodical are you?	. . . . .
How ruthless are you?	. . . . .
Subtotal 1	. . . . .
Plus starter points	. 100 .
Subtotal 2	. . . . .

Next, add up your scores from the following questionnaires:

How obsessive are you?	. . . . .
How dominating are you?	. . . . .
Subtotal 3	. . . . .

Subtract Subtotal 3 from Subtotal 2.

Total   . . . . .

CAREER GUIDANCE CLINIC 3

Begin by giving yourself 50 points.

Now, add up your scores from the following question-naires:

Are you a doer or a thinker?
How inquisitive are you?
How practical are you?
How methodical are you?
Subtotal 1
Plus starter points   50
Subtotal 2
Next, record your score from the following questionnaire:
How obsessive are you?
This is Subtotal 3.
Subtract Subtotal 3 from Subtotal 2.
Total

CAREER GUIDANCE CLINIC 4

Add up your scores from the following questionnaires:

How imaginative are you?
How emotional are you?
How artistic are you?
How much of an individual are you?
How sensual are you?
Total

CAREER GUIDANCE CLINIC 5

Begin by giving yourself 50 points.

Now, add up your scores from the following question-naires:

How responsible are you? . . . . .
How methodical are you? . . . . .
How thrifty are you? . . . . .
How stubborn are you? . . . . .
Subtotal 1 . . . . .
Plus starter points . 50 .
Subtotal 2 . . . . .
Next, record your score from the following questionnaire:
How obsessive are you? . . . . .
This is Subtotal 3. . . . .
Subtract Subtotal 3 from Subtotal 2.
Total . . . . .

In order to compare your scores in these five separate Clinics you must now add leveling figures to your original scores.

Clinic	Original score	Add	Total
1	. . . . .	80	. . . . .
2	. . . . .	15	. . . . .
3	. . . . .	55	. . . . .
4	. . . . .	55	. . . . .
5	. . . . .	70	. . . . .

The five totals that you now have will enable you to select the type of career for which you are best suited. Simply pick the clinic for which you have the highest total and consult the following table to find out what sort of job is right for you.

CLINIC 1

If your highest score was in Clinic 1, you are best suited for a job that involves caring for people. Suitable jobs might include: doctor, dentist, nurse, psychologist, social worker, health visitor, teacher, lecturer, physiotherapist, dietician, chiropodist, radiographer, speech therapist, optician.

CLINIC 2

If your highest score was in Clinic 2, you are best suited for a job that involves organizing or influencing people. Suitable jobs might include: security work, sales and representation, market research, management, police work, military work.

CLINIC 3

If your highest score was in Clinic 3, you are best suited for a job in engineering, science or research. Suitable jobs might include work in civil, mechanical, electrical or chemical engineering. If you scored high on the questionnaire headed "How inquisitive are you?", a job in research would be particularly suitable.

CLINIC 4

If your highest score was in Clinic 4, you are best suited for a job that involves work in communications, the media or the visual arts. If you prefer working with words rather than pictures, you might consider the following occupations: journalism, public relations, advertising, translation. If you prefer working with pictures rather than words, then consider graphic design, interior design, architecture, fashion design, photography, window display, theater design.

CLINIC 5

If your highest score was in Clinic 5, you are best suited for a job that involves administration. If you prefer working with numbers rather than words, then select from this list: accounting, banking, computer programming, systems analysis. If, however, you prefer working with words rather than numbers, then select from this list: civil service, the law, library work, record keeping, research administration, secretarial.

Could you run your own business?

Begin by giving yourself 100 points.

Now, add up your score from the following questionnaires:

Are you a doer or a thinker?   . . . . .
How daring are you?   . . . .

How ambitious are you? . . . . . .

Are you a workaholic? . . . . .

Subtotal 1 . . . . .

Plus starter points . 100 .

Subtotal 2 . . . . .

Next, add your score from the following questionnaires:

How obsessive are you? . . . . .

How dominating are you? . . . . .

Have you got your priorities right? . . . . .

Subtotal 3 . . . . .

To find out if you could run your own business subtract Subtotal 2 from Subtotal 3.

Total . . . . .

If you scored between 125 and 180, you stand a marvelous chance of running your own business successfully and profitably. You have all the necessary qualities for self-employed success.

If you scored between 78 and 124, you would probably be able to make a success of being your own boss, but perhaps you should think carefully before setting up as an entrepreneur.

If you scored 77 or less, you would be well advised to remain on the company payroll. Your psychological status does not suggest that you would make a successful self-employed business person.

How well would you cope if you were shipwrecked— would you survive on a desert island?

Add together your scores from the following questionnaires:

How optimistic are you?	. . . .
How strong is your self-image?	. .
How daring are you?	.
How practical are you?	. .
How methodical are you?	. . .
How much of an individual are you?	. . .
Total	. . .

If you scored between 98 and 135, you are a real survivor. The chances are excellent that you would survive on a desert island.

If you scored between 38 and 97, you'd probably struggle a bit. You'd have great difficulty in coping with some of the problems you faced and you would possibly get close to despair. But you'd survive.

If you scored 37 or less, I suggest that you take great care while traveling by sea. Always stay close to someone who looks like a real survivor. Do your best to keep away from desert islands.

Are you a wimp or a bully?

Begin by giving yourself 100 points.

Now, add up your scores from the following questionnaires:

How assertive are you?	. . . . .
How daring are you?	. . . . .
How ruthless are you?	. . . . .
Subtotal 1	. . . . .
Plus starter points	. 100 .
Subtotal 2	. . . . .

Next, add up your scores from the following questionnaires:

How absent-minded are you?	. . . . .
How dominating are you?	. . . . .
Are you indecisive?	. . . . .
Subtotal 3	. . . . .

To find out if you are a wimp or a bully subtract Subtotal 3 from Subtotal 2.

Total	. . . . .

If you scored between 141 and 185, you are strong-willed and firm-minded. You know what you want and how to get it, and, if necessary, you'll take chances. Some people may think of you as something of a bully.

If you scored between 90 and 140, you have a broad spread of natural skills and qualities. You respond in different ways to different problems and different people. When necessary you can be firm, but deep down you're soft-hearted.

If you scored 89 or less, you are shy, cautious and reluctant to assert yourself. You are definitely a follower rather than a leader. You are, I fear, something of a wimp.

How creative are you?

Add up your scores from the following questionnaires:

How intuitive are you?
How imaginative are you?
How emotional are you?
How inquisitive are you?
How artistic are you?
How much of an individual are you?
How sensual are you?
Total

If you scored between 69 and 130, you have an extremely creative and inventive mind.

If you scored between 27 and 68, you are capable of having original ideas but, on the whole, you prefer to get on with life as it is.

If you scored 26 or less, you are not particularly creative, though you may, occasionally, have some very good ideas.

Are you the sort who falls in love easily?

Add up your scores from the following questionnaires:

How imaginative are you?   . . . . .
How emotional are you?   . . . . .
How strong is your sex drive?   . . . . .
How romantic are you?   . . . . .
How sensual are you?   . . . . .
How impulsive are you?   . . . . .
Total   . . . . .

If you scored between 66 and 120, you are constantly in love—if you ever fall out of love, within minutes you'll be back in love again! You are wildly and gloriously romantic and impulsive. And, to a certain extent, you're in love with being in love.

If you scored between 25 and 65, your real loves are few and far between. You rarely really let yourself go—though when you do fall in love, it may be something rather special.

If you scored 24 or less, you are far too practical and sensible to be forever falling in love.

Would you make a successful criminal?

Begin by giving yourself 100 points.

Now, add up your scores from the following questionnaires:

Are you a doer or a thinker?

How daring are you?

How ambitious are you?

How methodical are you?

How ruthless are you?

Subtotal 1

Plus starter points   100

Subtotal 2

Next, add your score from the following questionnaires:

How vulnerable are you to guilty feelings?

How honorable are you?

How trusting are you?

Subtotal 3

To find out whether or not you would make a successful criminal subtract Subtotal 3 from Subtotal 2.
Total

If you scored between 154 and 195, you would probably make a very successful criminal. You have all the necessary qualities—coolness, ruthlessness and daring. Equally important, you are unencumbered with such emotional baggage as guilt, honor and trust.

If you scored between 91 and 153, you *might* make a successful criminal, but the odds are against you.

If you scored 90 or less, you must simply accept that you just don't have what it takes to become a successful criminal. The lower your score, the more likely you are to end up in prison.

Are you a good lover?

Begin by giving yourself 100 points.

Now, add up your scores from the following questionnaires:

How loyal are you?
How imaginative are you?

How emotional are you?   . . . . .
How daring are you?   . . . . .
How strong is your sex drive?   . . . . .
How romantic are you?   . . . . .
How sensual are you?   . . . . .
How good is your sense of humor?   . . . . .
Subtotal 1   . . . . .
Plus starter points   . 100 .
Subtotal 2   . . . . .
Next, add your score from the following questionnaires:
Are you jealous?   . . . . .
How prudish are you?   . . . . .
Are you liberated?   . . . . .
Subtotal 3   . . . . .
To find out how good a lover you are subtract Subtotal 3 from
Subtotal 2.
Total   . . . . .

If you scored between 193 and 270, you are a wonderful
lover, gentle but exciting, loving and loyal, imaginative but
thoughtful.

If you scored between 116 and 192, you have most of the
necessary qualities to become a good lover. To put yourself
into the superlover class you perhaps need to let yourself go
a little more; let your imagination and your senses take control.

If you scored 115 or less, then, although you may love and
be loved, you are not, I fear, a candidate for immortality as
one of the world's great lovers.

Are you the type to have a secret affair?

Begin by giving yourself 200 points.

Now, add up your scores from the following questionnaires:

How emotional are you?
How daring are you?
How strong is your sex drive?
How romantic are you?
How impulsive are you?
Subtotal 1
Plus starter points   200
Subtotal 2
Next, add up your scores from the following questionnaires:
How much of a worrier are you?
How responsible are you?
How vulnerable are you to guilty feelings?
Subtotal 3
To find out if you are the type who could have a secret affair
subtract Subtotal 3 from Subtotal 2.
Total

If you scored between 259 and 315, you have all the qualities you need to have a successful secret affair. You're lusty,

daring, impulsive and you fall in love easily. More important, perhaps, you can have an affair without worrying about it too much.

If you scored between 191 and 258, you might fancy an affair, and you'd certainly enjoy one. But even if your strong inhibitions and guilt feelings don't hold you back, they'll make you suffer for your indiscretion.

If you scored 190 or less, you really should forget all about having an affair. For you, the pain and the sorrow will certainly outweigh any fleeting joy.

Do you stand out in a crowd?

Begin by giving yourself 100 points.

Now, add up your scores from the following questionnaires:

How assertive are you? . . . . .
Are you a doer or a thinker? . . . . .
How emotional are you? . . . . .
How strong is your self-image? . . . . .
How daring are you? . . . . .
How irascible are you? . . . . .
How artistic are you? . . . . .

How much of an individual are you? . . . .

How impulsive are you? . . . .

How good is your sense of humor? . . .

Subtotal 1 . .

Plus starter points . 100 .

Subtotal 2 . .

Next, record your score from the following questionnaire:

How dominating are you? . .

This is Subtotal 3. . .

To find out if you stand out in a crowd subtract Subtotal 3 from Subtotal 2.

Total .

If you scored between 239 and 335, you are truly the life and soul of any party. Your presence is always noticeable and memorable.

If you scored between 142 and 238, you *can* stand out in a crowd—but it all depends on how you feel: sometimes you sparkle, sometimes you don't.

If you scored 141 or less, you are the wallflower type. You'd probably feel desperately embarrassed—and go bright red— if anyone noticed you.

How reliable are you?

Add up your scores from the following questionnaires:

How responsible are you?   . . . . .
How loyal are you?   . . . . .
How methodical are you?   . . . . .
How good is your memory?   . . . . .
How honorable are you?   . . . . .
Are you a workaholic?   . . . . .
Total   . . . . .

If you scored between 57 and 95, you are utterly reliable and trustworthy.

If you scored between 24 and 56, you are fairly reliable, although you do occasionally let people down.

If you scored 23 or less, then, although you may mean well and may intend to keep your promises, you would probably be the first to admit that you are not really the reliable sort. Perhaps "unpredictable" would be a more acceptable and accurate description!

Could you run the country?

Begin by giving yourself 50 points.

Now, add up your scores from the following questionnaires:

How assertive are you?
How strong is your self-image?
How ambitious are you?
How ruthless are you?
How stubborn are you?
Are you a workaholic?
Subtotal 1
Plus starter points   50
Subtotal 2
Next, add up your scores from the following questionnaires:
How dominating are you?
Are you indecisive?
Subtotal 3
To find out if you could run the country subtract Subtotal 3
from Subtotal 2.
Total

If you scored between 125 and 190, you would make an excellent job of running the country. You have all the essential qualities.

If you scored between 60 and 124, you could probably manage to run the country successfully, but your health would suffer and I doubt if you'd really like the job (however attractive it might sound at a distance).

If you scored 59 or less, you should definitely let someone else run the country—you have few (if any) of the essential attributes for national leadership.

Have you got what it takes to become a film star?

Begin by giving yourself 100 points.

Now, add up your scores from the following questionnaires:

How strong is your self-image?	. . . . .
How ambitious are you?	. . . . .
How artistic are you?	. . . . .
How much of an individual are you?	. . . . .
How vain are you?	. . . . .
Subtotal 1	. . . . .
Plus starter points	. 100 .
Subtotal 2	. . . . .

Next, add up your scores from the following questionnaires:

How dominating are you?   . . . . .

Have you got your priorities right?   . . . . .

Subtotal 3   . . . . .

To find out if you've got what it takes to become a film star subtract Subtotal 3 from Subtotal 2.

Total   . . . . .

If you scored between 152 and 200, you can start organizing the fan club now. You've got all the qualities needed for stardom. The only other ingredients you need are a pinch of talent and a bucketful of luck.

If you scored between 100 and 151, you've got most of the qualities you need to become a film star, but it's going to be really hard work and you could well get badly hurt on the way. It goes without saying that if you're going to succeed, you'll need some talent and an extraordinary amount of good luck.

If you scored 99 or less, you weren't made for stardom. You certainly wouldn't like the climb upward, and you probably wouldn't enjoy being a star if you did manage to get there.

Are you likely to reach the top in a company hierarchy?

Begin by giving yourself 100 points.

Now, add up your scores from the following questionnaires:

How responsible are you?
How loyal are you?
How ambitious are you?
How ruthless are you?
How stubborn are you?
Are you a workaholic?
Subtotal 1
Plus starter points   100
Subtotal 2
Next, add up your scores from the following questionnaires:
How obsessive are you?
How much of an individual are you?
Have you got your priorities right?
Subtotal 3
To find out whether or not you are likely to reach the top in a company hierarchy subtract Subtotal 3 from Subtotal 2.
Total

If you scored between 143 and 195, you are destined for the top. You have what it takes to rise in a company hierarchy and you could reach the boardroom without any difficulty at all.

If you scored between 63 and 142, you could fight your way to the top—but it will be a long, hard battle that will involve many sacrifices on your part. And there will be a few wounds on the way too.

If you scored 62 or less, you would probably be wise to remain content to stay where you are. You do not have the psychological make-up to claw your way upward without suffering great injuries.

What sort of patient would you make?

Begin by giving yourself 20 points.

Now, add up your scores from the following questionnaires:

How much of a worrier are you?	. . . . .
How imaginative are you?	. . . . .
Are you a hypochondriac?	. . . . .
Are you a positive or negative thinker?	. . . . .
Subtotal 1	. . . . .

Plus starter points   . . 20
Subtotal 2   . . .
Next, record your score from the following questionnaire:
How stubborn are you?
This is Subtotal 3.
To find out what sort of patient you would make
subtract Subtotal 3 from Subtotal 2.
Total   . .

If you scored between 61 and 115, you would make a terrible patient—constantly worrying about your health, forever
convinced that something terrible is going to happen to you.

If you scored between 33 and 60, you are a pretty average
sort of patient. Your natural concern for your own good health
is tempered by your determination to put a brave face on
things. Determined not to make too much fuss, you tend to
worry in silence.

If you scored 32 or less, you are an excellent patient—you
cope bravely with your ailments, never making an unreason-
able fuss and always looking on the bright side.

Could you succeed in politics?

Begin by giving yourself 50 points.

Now, add up your scores from the following questionnaires:

How sociable are you? . . . . .
How assertive are you? . . . . .
How strong is your self-image? . . . . .
How ambitious are you? . . . . .
How ruthless are you? . . . . .
How vain are you? . . . . .
Subtotal 1 . . . . .
Plus starter points . . 50 .
Subtotal 2 . . . . .
Next, record your score from the following questionnaire:
How dominating are you? . . . . .
This is Subtotal 3.
To find out if you could succeed in politics subtract Subtotal 3 from Subtotal 2.
Total . . . . .

If you scored between 147 and 200, you should seriously consider a career in politics. You seem to have all the necessary attributes!

If you scored between 74 and 146, you might be able to succeed in politics, but you will have to work hard to use those skills that you have. If you are not committed or dedicated to a particular cause, you should perhaps turn your attentions elsewhere.

If you scored 73 or less, you are not the type for an active role in politics. Your gentle, self-effacing, modest nature would not serve you well in the hurly-burly of political life.

How good are you with children?

Begin by giving yourself 20 points.

Now, add up your scores from the following questionnaires:

How sociable are you?
How imaginative are you?
How kind are you?
How stubborn are you?
Subtotal 1
Plus starter points   20
Subtotal 2
Next, record your score from the following questionnaire:

How tolerant are you?   . . . . .
This is Subtotal 3.
To find out how good you are with children subtract Subtotal
3 from Subtotal 2.
Total   . . . . .

If you scored between 61 and 95, you are wonderful with
children.

If you scored between 28 and 60, you're good with children, although your patience is not unlimited.

If you scored 27 or less, your affection for children—particularly other people's children—is probably limited by your
lack of tolerance and patience.

Will you ever be rich?

Begin by giving yourself 200 points.

Add your scores from the following questionnaires:

How assertive are you?   . . . . .
Are you a doer or a thinker?   . . . . .
How strong is your self-image?   . . . . .
How daring are you?   . . . . .

How ambitious are you?   . . .
How ruthless are you?   . . . . .
How thrifty are you?   . . .
Are you a workaholic?   . . .
Subtotal 1   . . .
Plus starter points   . 200
Subtotal 2
Now, add together your scores from the following question-
naires:
How obsessive are you?   . . .
How dominating are you?   . . .
How content are you?   . . .
Have you got your priorities right?
Subtotal 3   . .
To find out if you will ever be rich subtract Subtotal 3 from
Subtotal 2.
Total   . . .

If you scored between 295 and 390, your chances of be-
coming extremely rich are excellent. You have all the necessary qualities. Now all you need is luck!

If you scored between 197 and 294, there is a good chance
that you will be rich one day. However, you enjoy life too
much to be single-minded in your pursuit of wealth.

If you scored 196 or less, you are, I fear, unlikely ever to
be rich. But you must balance this disappointment with the
knowledge that you will probably get more pleasure and fun
out of life than many millionaires. And you could always win
a lottery!

What sort of partner is right for you?

To find out what sort of partner is right for you simply check through your score in the following questionnaires:

HOW SOCIABLE ARE YOU?

If you scored high on this questionnaire and you enjoy meeting people and going to parties, you probably need a partner with similar tastes who also scores high on this questionnaire. If one of you constantly wants to stay at home and the other constantly wants to go out dancing and drinking, there could be conflict.

HOW ASSERTIVE ARE YOU?

If you are extremely assertive and your partner is assertive too, then your relationship is bound to be an explosive one, with plenty of arguments and rows. The happiest relationship may well be one in which one partner is assertive and the other is not.

ARE YOU A DOER OR A THINKER?

In an ideal relationship at least one partner will be a doer rather than a thinker. If you are both dreamers and thinkers, nothing will ever get done.

HOW AMBITIOUS ARE YOU?

If you are ambitious and your partner is not, that could be a recipe for disaster. Your ambitions and plans for the future need to be in harmony if your relationship is to last.

HOW IRASCIBLE ARE YOU?

If you are both short-tempered and easily roused, your relationship will be a stormy one.

HOW STRONG IS YOUR SEX DRIVE?

If one of you has a powerful sex drive and the other is more interested in gardening, the future will not be a happy one.

HOW MUCH OF AN INDIVIDUAL ARE YOU?

If you are both strong-willed individuals, you will probably take some time to create a real partnership. However, when you have developed a proper partnership, you will probably be unable to cope without one another.

ARE YOU JEALOUS?

One jealous partner can lead to friction. Two jealous partners can lead to disaster.

ARE YOU INDECISIVE?

If both of you are indecisive, it could lead to problems. One of you really needs to be able to make decisions. But remember that if you are both decisive, that could lead to problems too—unless you both make the same decisions!

HOW THRIFTY ARE YOU?

Arguments about money cause more trouble than disagreements about sex. Either one of you needs to control the purse strings or else you need to formulate a common monetary policy.

HOW VAIN ARE YOU?

If you both are vain, then you need two bathrooms in order to have a happy relationship.

These are, of course, just some of the personality facets that can lead to possible problems within a relationship. If you check through the other questionnaires in this book, you'll soon find other conclusions that will give you food for thought. Once you've completed all the questionnaires, get your partner to do the same, and then compare scores. You'll be amazed at what you discover about one another.

About the Author

Vernon Coleman is a best-selling British author who writes mainly on the subject of medicine. He is a qualified doctor (what we would call an M.D.) and Fellow of the Royal Society of Medicine. Dr. Coleman lives on the north Devon coast.